365

DAYS OF
COLOUR
IN YOUR GARDEN

365 DAYS OF COLOUR IN YOUR GARDEN

NICK BAILEY

Photography by Jonathan Buckley

KYLE BOOKS

CONTENTS

As a gardener I savour the

fleeting beauty and colours of plants. As the seasons rise, peak and fade so do the colour riches of a thoughtfully crafted garden. Vermillion and peach, lime and burnt orange all take their turn with the passing months, but dressing all 365 days of the year with bejewelled wonders is our greatest challenge as gardeners. Through experiment, observation, disaster and gentle pointers from plants themselves, I've come to understand some of the craft and cunning this pursuit requires.

The infinite variability of plant colour in the gardens I've tended and loved has surprised, delighted and humbled me. My earliest memories are strewn with wonderment at the ability of plants to conjure up a million different colours. My grandfather's daffodil-filled orchard and my mother's references to the mysterious-sounding raw umber and ultramarine blue in her paintbox initiated a love of colour that continues to grow.

And, of course, I'm not alone. Most of us crave colour in one way or another. The base or background colours of our world tend to be neutrals and often of their place – be that stone, brick, wood or soil. This neutrality can leave us somehow bereft. Spikes of colour grab our attention or set up a hierarchy of just what we should look at first when we enter a new environment. A garden may harbour untold horticultural treasures but it is nearly always the 'colour' that captures the attention of the people who visit it. History is full of such tales. The Dutch tulip crisis of the early 1600s, which all but crippled the economy of the Netherlands, happened as a result of the pursuit of colour. Colour is intrinsic to our lives and carries meaning, feeling and response with it. It's a cultural identifier in

our clothes, products, architecture and gardens. So strong is the palette used in India, for example, that colour is virtually a cultural export – think saris, spices and clouds of colourful powdered dye filling the air at celebrations. Japan cherishes a different palette; its buildings, clothes and consumables often tend towards pastels and neutral shades. Every country, town, village, house, garden and person has its own particular colours of choice that mark it out as individual.

Colour influences everything. It can determine the way we move, think and see ourselves. The same product, sold to men and women, may have a black or pink livery respectively to lure the sexes into consuming a product in 'their colour'. The messages and signals sent out by colour define us and often put us in boxes, but in the garden there is total freedom to play with colour in ways we may not consider appropriate to our homes, clothes or cars. Unlike these 'fixed' colours, the garden is in a perpetual state of colour flux. Designing with these ever-changing entities is arguably harder than with 'fixed' colours. So, with these challenges in mind we create our gardens. We are initiators of works of art, which take on their own life as plants and their surroundings interact with one another, the seasons, light and weather. We strive for longevity in colour, form and texture. And if we look hard enough we find that there is not only a plant for every day of the year but myriad plants capable of bringing changing colour to multiple seasons, or runs of flower and foliage that persist for months on end. These plants, carefully sited and placed with one another, become part of the ever-changing colours that fill the 365-day garden.

Top **Helleborus foetidus
'Wester Flisk' displays
numerous 'greens'
through the year.**

Bottom **This delicate
Ipheion is the result of
extensive breeding work.**

What do we mean by 'colour' in gardens?

When we talk about colour in gardens, more often than not we're referring to its flowers. But if you take a slice of the average garden the majority of its colour is contributed by leaves, stems and shadows; in other words, green. So abundant is this colour that we almost overlook its ever-changing qualities of tone and luminosity. Taking a closer look reveals hues, textures and subtleties of foliage tone. *Helleborus foetidus* 'Wester Flisk' is a case in point. Its evergreen foliage glides between richest dark greens and more glaucous blue-grey tones as the seasons change. This, coupled with red-brown stems that suffuse into the base of the leaves, makes for a plant rich in numerous tones that looks striking even without its fresh lime-green flowers. Other deciduous plants may take on innumerable colours as their leaves progress from pale spring green to dusty summer green, to the browns, reds, yellows and oranges of autumn. So long before we consider introducing 'colour', it's worth noting that it is already there as a subtle green canvas ready to be furnished with the stand-out hues of the flowers, stems and fruits we bring to it.

Man's influence on plant colour and longevity

The first cultivated ornamental plants emerged an extraordinary five thousand years ago in the East, particularly in China and India, where sustainable agriculture led to stable communities and the pursuit of beauty. Although some of these 'new' plants made their way to Europe, it was not until the sixteenth century, during the Renaissance, that these selected ornamental species began arriving in droves. Many had already been bred in the most rudimentary fashion or selected from batches for their vigour, health, longevity or colour.

Gregor Mendel's famous experiments of the mid-nineteenth century, involving crossing red and white peas, went some way to explaining genetic inheritance and how growers could actively affect plant characteristics. This has, of course, given rise to tens of thousands of new plants created or selected by Man. Nature can play its part, too. Natural mutations also occur in plants, giving rise to novel forms which may have qualities of colour or form suited to the garden. The Dutch, with their penchant for bulbs, led much breeding, spurred on by the quest for colour. Species that arrived in Renaissance Holland were grown, selected and bred. Tulips and hyacinths are prime examples from which thousands of coloured cultivars were developed and selected from a relatively small palette of original colours. Roses have a similar history. From less than 100 wild species, breeders across Asia, Europe and more recently the Americas have developed thousands of cultivars in myriad colours that don't exist in the wild.

Breeders have been driven by the quest for longevity, too. Crosses and selections of numerous plants have been made in order to create ever-longer-blooming plants. Roses, whose ancestors may have only flowered for a matter of weeks, now flower for months. Flowers are, of course, just one component of plant colour, with leaves, stems and fruits carrying colour for the lion's share of the year. This has led breeders to experiment with colour and longevity here, too, resulting in the plethora of rich-hued foliage plants such as heucheras, tiarellas and hostas, that have all arrived in recent years.

Colour woven through garden history

Gardens, and the plants they house, have evolved radically over the last five thousand years. Fashion, politics, faith and numerous other factors have influenced the design of gardens, leading to evolutions in their symbolism, the range of plants used and the approach to colour. Gardens of the East were the first to develop; they drew on a rich palette of native plants and were heavily influenced by faith and symbolism, with colour playing a significant part in this. As Europe embraced ornamental gardening at around the time of the Renaissance, new gardens sprung up around palaces, stately homes and universities. The academic institutions focused on cultivating rare and useful plants in their gardens with science, rather than art, dictating their layout. Palaces and stately homes took a very different approach; gardens created around these vast properties in Italy, France, England, Germany and Holland often sought to represent the owners' control and strident power over the landscape. Colour began to play its part here, as the often green and monochromatic gardens of hedges, paths and parterres had colourful plants or gravel added to them, highlighting the shapes created between hedge-drawn patterns. Though these bright colours continued to be used in the immediate vicinity of vast homes through much of the next few centuries, the wider landscapes of such houses began to change under the influence of designers such as Capability Brown and Humphry Repton. These English designers of the eighteenth and early nineteenth centuries advocated a more 'naturalistic' approach. Their rolling landscapes of clustered trees, lakes and follies relied mainly on form rather than colour for their impact and were the height of fashion for the upper classes.

Simultaneously, the much romanticised cottage gardens of the working classes were also developing. Though their evolution was led by their provision of food, gardeners did make space to celebrate a polychromatic jumble of colour-rich plants. The Victorians were the first to truly embrace garden colour on the grand scale and have it lead their approach to garden making. Out went the sober, subtle colours of the past centuries, to be replaced by violently bright bedding plants, roses and perennials. Alton Towers in Derbyshire, England, epitomised the Victorian approach. This landscape, which still exists in part today, was a crazy mash-up of colours and forms – almost a celebration of the bright, brash and bizarre which embraced every hue and new plant available.

Late nineteenth- and early twentieth-century garden design continued the Victorians' colour obsession, but with an increasingly more sophisticated approach to planting design. Among the early pioneers of this more considered approach to colour was the extraordinary Gertrude Jekyll. Many gardeners dismiss her work, which stretched to over 400 gardens, as pretty pastels and little else, but her approach was far more diverse and sophisticated. True, harmonious colours and graduations through particular hues were at the heart of her work, but these didn't stand alone; they were punctuated with contrast. Pale tones were added to rich saturated colours to 'balance' them, and bright colours to pales for focus and contrast. Schemes combining lime, orange, blue and yellow which would not look out of place in an experimental contemporary garden, were her stock in trade as much as safe pastels. She was far more outrageous with colour than the pastel brush she is

Top Coloured gravel added vibrancy to historic topiary plantings.

Bottom Gertrude Jekyll's pastel plantings regularly featured bright colours.

Top **Sissinghurst Castle – an icon of arts and crafts design.**

Bottom **Red borders at Hidcote Manor.**

often tarred with. Munstead Wood, Jekyll's house in Surrey, England, still stands today and some of her colour adventures have been recreated in its gardens.

Other English gardens established around this era include Hidcote Manor, in Gloucestershire, and Sissinghurst Castle, in Kent. Both designs were based on a series of rooms opening out into the wider landscape – and both were colour-led. Each garden contained vibrant long-season plantings dominated by roses, annuals and perennials, often arranged into colour themes, such as Sissinghurst's renowned white garden and Hidcote's red borders. Similar approaches were being adopted elsewhere in Europe but by the middle of the century one stand-out designer, operating in South America, pushed garden colour another step forward. Roberto Burle Marx, a landscape architect, artist and plantsman, created painterly landscapes on a huge scale. The public parks and private gardens he crafted relied on sumptuous, often hot, plant colours in huge swathes and drifts which illuminated his landscapes. These gardens were very much of their place and relied on many native plants but they were always dominated by his liberal use of vibrant colour.

Famed gardeners, too numerous to mention, have each had their influence on garden and colour fashion over the last 60 years but one outshines the rest – the late English gardener, Christopher Lloyd. His influence on gardeners and their approach to garden colour can't be underestimated. Thanks to his publications, which were informed by a lifetime of gardening, he spread the word that colour in the garden is not something to fear but rather to embrace and play with. This approach bore extraordinary dividends at his home Great Dixter, in East Sussex, England, where his

experimental colour plantings have captured the imagination of gardeners everywhere. Rather than follow rigid planting design formulas he ignored the rules and created plantings which were sometimes subtle, sometimes shocking, but always had colour as one of their primary drivers. Oranges combined with pinks and zingy limes paired with magentas have given licence to the next generation of gardeners to be bold with colour.

Colour in wild places

Long before any gardener had gathered and arranged plants into beds and borders, Mother Nature had bestowed the world with wild colour-rich landscapes. These natural floral phenomenons, which occur across the globe, can feel virtually garden-like in their richness, diversity and colour spectacle. At different times of year, swathes of the planet burst into bloom or develop seasonal colours so dramatic that enthusiasts from around the world flock to marvel at these bits of fleeting floral magic. Many parts of Japan are resplendent in colour through spring thanks to wild plums and cherries flanking mountainsides, valleys and public parks. Hues of the palest pink through to the richest magenta create a confluence of colours so delicious that locals and travellers alike wander in awe among the festooned branches. Later in spring, Europe's alpine meadows erupt in myriad colours in their hasty attempt to flower and set seed before the snows return. Come summer, South Africa takes its turn in the spotlight. Namaqualand, north of Cape Town, draws in travellers to wonder at the vast swathes of blue, orange and white daisies that illuminate the desert landscape. Blankets of colour run for tens of miles and single blocks of, say, blue or orange, can take up areas the size of a large village. Later, in autumn, North America has

Inspiring wild plant colours and combinations can be found everywhere, from the South African desert (above) to the woodlands of Vermont and New England in fall (right).

its moment in the sun. The northern US states of Vermont, Maine and New Hampshire have many bands of acid soil and, therefore, the natural forests develop strikingly hot colours as their leaves senesce into autumn. Travellers visiting these extraordinary forests of colour, which extend for hundreds of miles, are referred to by the locals as 'leaf-peepers' and websites run live updates of the latest colour developments and how to get the best view of them.

We truly hunger for colour – and these wild places have it in droves. They show us, on a giant scale, the way in which colours work together and how plants interact with one another, the season and their environment. These inspirational landscapes, coupled with ideas from the great gardens of the past and present, along with an ever expanding palette of plants, means we are better equipped than ever before to create richly-coloured 365-day gardens.

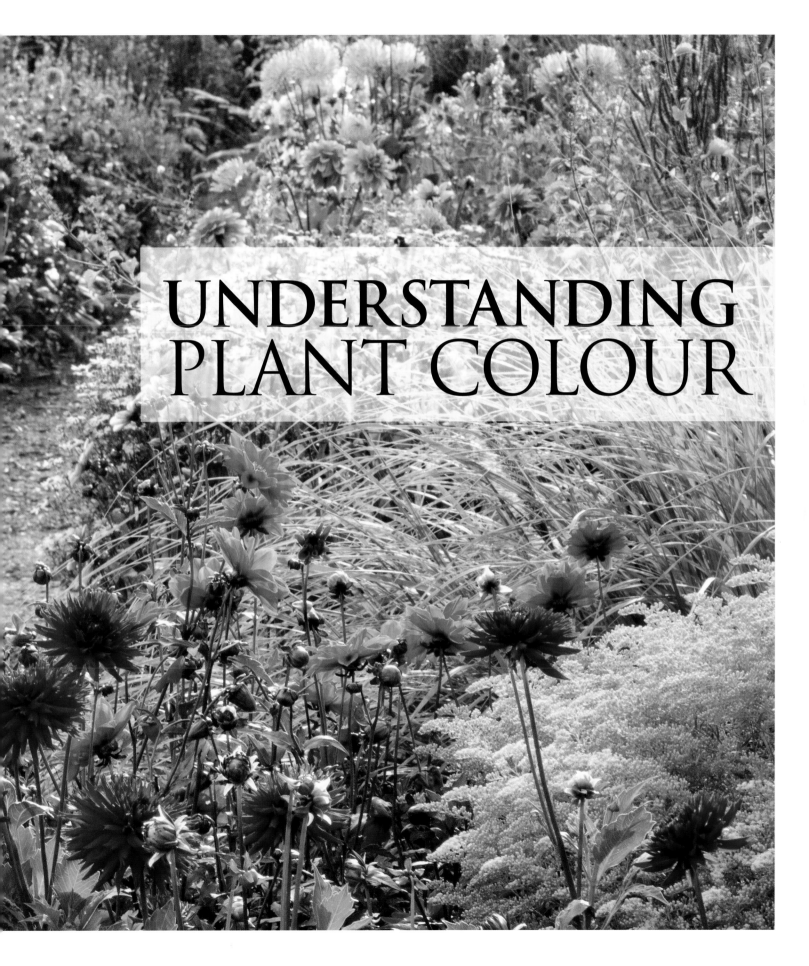

UNDERSTANDING
PLANT COLOUR

The ART and SCIENCE of PLANT COLOUR

The compounds and pigments found in plants reflect certain wavelengths of light from the sun, thus giving them their 'colour'.

What is colour?

All colours exist as a result of light, which is composed of different-coloured wavelengths. Sir Isaac Newton, of apple epiphany fame, established this by splitting light from the sun, through a prism, into its component parts of red, orange, yellow, green, blue, indigo and violet. This established that 'white' light from the sun was in fact a composite of many colours. Other components of light, such as ultraviolet and infrared, also sit within this composite of colours – known as the

electromagnetic spectrum – but are not visible to the human eye. Put simply, plant colour is based on the various coloured light wavelengths that are either reflected or absorbed by the pigments of plants (as with all colour). If a plant reflects wavelengths of red light, which has wave peaks averaging at around 0.0007mm, then the plant appears red. This is because the pigment in the plant reflects back the red light and absorbs all other light wavelengths. The red light then hits our eyes' retina and we 'see' red. Interesting stuff…

How plants make and use colour

Plants have various complex ways of producing colour by using minerals from the earth, water and sunlight. These colours are produced for many reasons; some are simply a consequence of plants' biological functions, others exist to deter or attract animals. Through some clever chemistry, plants are able to manufacture pigments such as carotenoids (for reds, oranges and browns), anthocyanins (magenta, blue and purple), anthoxanthins (strong yellow through to cream) and chlorophylls (all greens). These are held in either the cell sap, cell walls or protoplasm of the plant. In some instances, a plant may carry two or more pigments, giving rise to a further range of colours, such as mauves and purples.

Soil type can also affect the balance of pigments in plants, leading to the likes of hydrangeas developing blue flowers rather than pink in acid soil. True black does not exist in nature and can be defined only as the absence of light. However, a number of species could be called red-black or blue-black. These plants have either a greater density of dark pigment or several pigments mixed together. Plants of this colour reflect virtually no wavelength from the electromagnetic spectrum and therefore appear virtually black to the eye. White, too, can be formed in a number of different ways in plants. Some species make white pigments while others have air spaces in between cells and tissues which bounce light around, giving the impression of white. And, although we cannot see in ultraviolet, insects can, so some plants have evolved to reflect these rays to lure them in. Others rely on a wide range of flower colours to attract would-be pollinators to their blooms.

> *Buttercups have a layer of bright white granules below the flowers' pigment which bounces light back out of the petal.*

Petal texture can also play a role in a plant's colour 'effect'. Some dark-flowered species have developed fine patterns or protrusions on their petal surfaces which reflect light. The lustrous iridescent sheen of the near-black *Tulipa* 'Paul Scherer' is the result of fine grooves on its petals, like a CD. These rows of grooves cause light to bounce off them to dramatic effect. Buttercups and other 'glossy'-flowered plants have a similar trick; a layer of bright white starchy granules below the flowers' yellow pigment bounces light back out of the petal resulting in their familiar glossy blooms. Other colour 'effects' are created in different ways. Plants with grey, blue or silver foliage often owe their colouring to hairy, waxy or powdery coatings rather than pigment. These coatings, which cover otherwise green leaves, exist to protect plants from intense sunlight. Other leaf colourings, such as burgundy, rely on pigments. These are often so potent that they disguise the green chlorophyll beneath them in the leaf. Variegations or multi-tonal leaves rarely occur in the wild but when mutants are discovered, or are encouraged through breeding, new forms of leaf variegation appear. The phenomenon of variegation is caused by a number of factors. Some plants, such as *Chlorophytum comosum* 'Vittatum' (spider plant) simply have a lack of pigment (usually held in their chloroplasts), which leads to its white longitudinal stripes. Other patterns can also occur in some plants due to a combination of defective chloroplasts and supplemental blue or red anthocyanin pigments. Air trapped under the outer layer of cells can also create a variegated look. This occurs in plants such as *Pilea cadierei* – the aluminium plant. Viruses can also cause variegation.

Top left **Pigments create the 'greens' which furnish our gardens.** *Top right* **Reflective protrusions on Nicotiana.** *Bottom right* **The absense of leaf pigment leads to variegation.** *Bottom left* **A combination of air and pigments colour Strobilanthes dyerianus.**

The COLOUR WHEEL for GARDENERS

The colour wheel is a simple device employed by artists and designers. In essence, the colours of the visible electromagnetic spectrum are bent round into a circle. The wheel demonstrates the relationship between colours and can be a useful tool to help in deciding their composition in the garden. School days remind us that the three primary colours – red, yellow and blue – are the foundation of the colour wheel and can't be created by mixing other colours. Turned into pigment, these primary colours are theoretically capable of creating all the other colours in the visible spectrum (the colour wheel). In between the primary colours sit the secondary colours, which are composed of the combined primaries that are on either side of them. Between yellow and blue sits green, between red and yellow sits orange, and between red and blue sits violet.

Further colours, known as tertiary colours, are created when primary and secondary colours are mixed. For example, combining primary red with secondary violet creates a red-violet, better known as

magenta. Of course, this does not generate all colours on Earth, or even in the garden. Numerous shades, tints and tones are generated by adding black and/or white pigment to a pure colour. By progressively adding more white to pure red it becomes an ever paler pink. Conversely, by adding black to pure red it becomes ever darker.

Artists and designers use several terms to describe colour. Temperature refers to colours relative warmth or coolness; reds and oranges are 'warm', whereas blues and greens are 'cool'. This is an easy concept to understand but other terms such as 'hue', 'value' and 'chroma' are not in most of our day-to-day lexicons. Put simply, 'value' refers to a colour's lightness or darkness, 'chroma' (used interchangeably with 'saturation') to a colour's intensity or vibrancy, and 'hue' just refers to a colour such as blue. Being aware of these terms and how the colour wheel works is by no means essential to being a good 365-day gardener, but it can help in making the right colour choices for your plot.

Clockwise from top
Muted or saturated
versions of the
primary colours
create dramatic
planting combinations.

Near-black plants
occur as a result of
high levels of red and/
or blue pigments in
their cells.

A range of yellow hues
sit comfortably
alongside one another
both on the colour
wheel and in this
planting.

This elegant planting hangs together as a result of combining ever paler versions of yellow-green in the leaves, stems and flowers of the Petunia, Nicotiana and Cleome.

Using the colour wheel to create effective colour combinations

The colour wheel is far from the be-all and end-all when it comes to understanding and using colour but it does provide some safe frameworks and pairings that will guarantee success. I use these combinations for particular effect but I'm equally likely to throw out the rule book and try all sorts of other combinations.

MONOCHROMATIC COMBINATIONS

These simple groupings see a range of shades and tints of one pure colour placed together. A simple monochrome colour scheme would see pure blue combined with lighter and darker shades of itself. Pairing *Veronica gentianoides*, *Delphinium* 'Blue Jay', *Ceanothus* 'Concha' and *Delphinium* 'Blue Butterfly' could create this scheme. Such a planting certainly hangs together but it would be potentially dull without contrasts in form and texture to balance its 'sameness'.

Colour combinations that don't follow the 'rules' of the colour wheel such as this pairing of Salvia and Coreopsis, open up a new palette of daring possibilities.

Shade and tints of a single colour, such as blue, sit harmoniously together as demonstrated in this understated border.

The slightly muted colours of this campanula and salvia sit side by side on the colour wheel making them a comfortable colour pairing.

ANALOGOUS COMBINATIONS

Schemes based on this formulation combine colours that are next to each other on the colour wheel, for example, red-orange, orange and yellow-orange. This is a safe bet and is sure to generate harmonious schemes with just a dash of excitement. Pairing *Pilosella aurantiaca*, *Calendula officinalis* and *Geum* 'Georgenberg' demonstrates the appeal of this combination. Using colours of the same value balances the scheme, preventing any one colour from dominating.

Dramatic colour contrasts can be achieved by pairing colours from opposite sides of the colour wheel. Yellow and purple set one another off (above) while orange and blue together positively glow (left). Red and green combinations work to similar effect.

CONTRASTING/COMPLIMENTARY COMBINATIONS

Pairing colours from opposite sides of the colour wheel guarantees rich, saturated, vibrant contrasts such as purple and yellow, red and green, or orange and blue. This easy formula is a sure-fire way of creating drama. Plantings such as *Achillea* 'Terracotta' and *Aconitum carmichaelii* (Wilsonii Group) (see page 147) are a case in point. The visual phenomenon known as simultaneous contrast comes into play here. The science is a little heavy but in essence it means that as the eye moves between contrasting colours they both become more intense as a result of their proximity to each other.

Veronica, Phlox and Lysimachia carry muted hues of the three primary colours, creating a triadic combination. A trio of purple, green and orange or blue-green, yellow-orange and red-purple work to similar effect.

TRIADIC COMBINATIONS

Often favoured by florists, a triadic or three-colour scheme takes colours evenly spaced around the colour wheel and places them together. It creates more complex combinations of colour than a contrasting scheme and often sees one colour dominate. For example, using blue-green, yellow-orange and red-violet together works a treat, but the red does dominate.

66 *Favoured by florists, a three-colour scheme takes colours evenly spaced around the colour wheel and places them together.* 99

NEUTRAL COMBINATIONS

If you were to create a series of concentric circles inside the colour wheel, with each displaying ever lighter shades and tints of the original pure colours, you'd have generated a neutral palette. In other words, a series of washed-out pastel versions of every colour. Red becomes palest pink, green becomes white with a green tint, and so on. This range of colours sits easily together without any particular one dominating the scene. This scheme could be created by pairing *Kniphofia* 'Little Maid', *Clematis florida* var. *flore-pleno* and *Lavatera maritima*.

The intense hues of this Dahlia and Alstroemeria carry equal colour 'weighting' therefore balancing each other's drama.

Pale pastel groupings sit easily together without a particular shade or tint dominating.

SATURATED COMBINATIONS

Using colours with full chroma (saturation) is essentially about combining any number of pure colours from the colour wheel. This can lead to highly dramatic and visually striking schemes, but throwing all these hues together could result in a polychromatic confluence of colours that is potentially overwhelming – think Victorian bedding schemes. Mixing up *Rudbeckia* var. *sullivantii* 'Goldsturm', *Salvia patens*, *Lobelia cardinalis* 'Bee's Flame' and an orange hemerocallis would result in a saturated kaleidoscopic mix that's sure to stop you in your tracks.

COLOUR THEORY *in the* GARDEN

Plant colours can be brought to life, muted or overlooked depending on how they are combined.

It is impossible to talk about combining plant colours in absolute terms. There are so many nuances and variables that stem from the season, the light and the time of day to the effects of other nearby colours and everyone's differing perception. The key principles, however, behind colour theory can be applied in the garden to great effect. It can guide decisions or lead to an understanding of why colours work together or which colours may need to be parachuted in to bring a planting scheme to life.

I find myself comparing colours and their relationships wherever I am. Initial observations of striking or subtle pairs are often rooted in colour theory principles, which can work as a reliable guide when beginning an adventure in garden colour. The diagram (opposite) illustrates some of the profound effects that colours have on one another. A colour can be 'warmed' by placing a cool colour next to it, or be brightened with the addition of a muted colour. Further profound colour relationships are shown in what is known as the Bezold Effect. Here, as illustrated in the image (right), the addition of white plants to a dark base colour radically changes our perception of it. This idea can be translated into most gardens with relative ease and can alter the essence of a whole planting scheme – one-time artist Gertrude Jekyll used it in her planting designs. For example, dotting silver-leaved shrubs through a planting lightens the overall effect and causes the existing colours to feel lighter and paler. Conversely, adding a dark foliage plant enhances the existing richer shades, making them appear more saturated. Jekyll also used the idea of optical mixing in her schemes – a principle identified by artists of the Impressionist era. Put simply, small yellow and blue dots on a canvas converge at a distance and read to our eye as green. Jekyll played with this idea to ease colour transitions and unify schemes.

The major difference between the artists' canvas, where many of these theories were formed, and the garden is of course light. Its effects on colour cannot be understated. A single flower, irrespective of its hue, can apparently glide between many different shades during the course of a single day. Blooms may appear muted at dawn, washed out at midday and rich in twilight, which adds another layer of complexity to combining colours. It's also worth considering which colours 'work' best in different countries, types of light and season. Harsh overhead midday light in the tropics and Mediterranean regions wash out paler colours but make bright, saturated hues positively glow. Rich colours that could look odd in murky northern European winters look beautiful in the low golden light of autumn. Attention to these effects and the guiding principles of colour theory can lead to beautiful planting schemes.

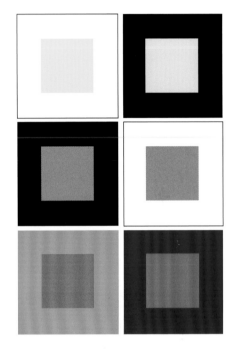

Forsythia and Ribes make for an eye wateringly bright spring combination.

That said, equally extraordinary groupings of colour may bear no relationship to any artistic theory, but it's surprising how many do. Classic garden colour combinations, such as apricot-pink roses grown with *Lavandula angustifolia*, correlate with colour theory. This pairing is essentially triadic; in other words it puts together three equidistant colours from the wheel: red-orange, yellow-green and blue-violet. They are not in their pure saturated states, of course, the rose is a pale red-orange with green foliage and the lavender a pale blue-violet with grey foliage. It makes for a satisfy combo because three of the four colours (blue-violet, red-orange and grey) are equally muted shades while the green provides a more saturated counterpoint and enlivens the pale trio. Other classic garden combinations, such as dark-pink *Ribes sanguineum* and mid-orange-yellow Forsythia are a bit shouty, to my mind, but they certainly do battle with late-winter's grey, life-sucking light. Their pairing bears no relation to the colour wheel but it's undoubtedly eye-catching.

Certain colour pairings only work because of a subtle nuance in shade. I find light pinks feel sickly next to certain mid-yellows, but if the yellow veers towards light yellow-green, such as the bracts and flowers of *Euphorbia characias*, then the pairing feels fresh and exciting – think big, blowsy light-pink roses with the yellow-green flowers of *Alchemilla mollis*. The success of such a pair is likely due to them being lightened versions of red and green (opposites on the colour wheel) and therefore complimentary (or contrasting). In their pure forms, red and green – such as the leaves and berries of holly – are even more intense as a result of them being dead opposite each other on the colour wheel.

Every nuance of shade or tint can make a difference when it comes to plant colour. The dark-violet flowers of a favourite trailing verbena of mine rely on a small flush of pale light violet at their throats. It's tiny, just millimetres wide, but it punctuates the centre of the flower enough to prevent the cluster of 20 or so dark-violet blooms melding into an amorphous blob, which, in all but the most intense light, could be dark and lifeless. Placed next to yellow *Solidago canadensis* the pair dramatically demonstrate that the base principles of colour theory hold true. Their two hues, dark-violet and yellow, (opposite each other on the wheel) suddenly radiate saturation in an almost alarming manner. They enliven and brighten each other. The same dark-violet verbena placed next to an orange hemerocallis appears to change colour again. This dark bloom, which could all but disappear in the shadows, suddenly glows with a redness that is virtually invisible against the yellow of the solidago.

Seasonal light and the time of day also make a huge difference to how colours appear. Backlit, the verbena takes on a whole new life. The bluey-hued pigments of anthocyanin dominate, giving the petals a strongly saturated violet colour with distinctly bluey hues. Exposed to midday sun the flowers are perhaps at their most defined and are colour-rich enough not to be bleached by the strong overhead light. Come twilight they disappear without a trace, while flowers with pale tints of their own violet hues almost emit light as they reflect it back from the moon's ethereal glow. Back in the light of day, the verbena flower takes on further chameleon qualities next to the pale light violet of a wild thistle, *Cirsium arvense*. The thistle's colour is a paled-down shade of the verbena. This highlights the verbena's pale throat with a near perfect colour match, giving the pair a strong colour relationship – they fit because the petals are monochromatic tints and shades, from the same family of colours, just lighter and darker than each other. Placing the pale thistle flowers next to a series of other colours demonstrates some surprising relationships. Against the orange

hemerocallis it looks washed out and wan. These colours sit nearly opposite on the colour wheel so they should zing, but because one, the thistle, is a dramatically pale shade of light violet it does not have enough clout to contrast with the hemerocallis, making it look wishy-washy – and it doesn't do the hemerocallis any favours either. Plucking a petal from the centre of the hemerocallis reveals a significantly paler version of the rest of the flower. It has a similar 'value' to the thistle's light-violet hue and paired together they create a lovely, gentle, possibly feminine feel. The colours are paled-down shades of colours that are near opposite on the wheel. Instead of the intense contrast of the verbena and solidago, this is a contrast of greater subtlety.

Reds of many shades can have a dramatic impact in the garden. They sit opposite green (the garden's most dominant colour) on the colour wheel and therefore contrast with everything that surrounds them. Introducing other colours to red is something I've always found a challenge. The yellow leaves of a golden privet placed next to the petals of a dark purple-red pelargonium look shocking. They are effectively one third of the colour wheel away from each other so their relationship is not clear. They fight, but it's more gentlemen-with-white-cotton-gloves than a bar brawl. It's exciting. Adding the colour that sits in the void between them – orange – in the form of a crocosmia flower, suddenly bonds the relationship. It's rich and overwhelming, which is no bad thing when we're looking for hot, vibrant groupings. This trio is simply analogous colours (those that sit next to each other on the wheel) harmonising.

Moving to the blues, it's notable how few plants carry this colour in its purest form.

Most have a tint of pink, red or purple to them. A late-flowering campanula, of unsure parentage, which I've just been wandering around the garden with, is a case in point. Next to the light pink petals of various roses and salvias it blushes with a subtle pink through its bluey hues, but next to orange hemerocallis or the mid-green foliage of various shrubs it's much closer to a true blue. Placed with its triadic buddies, pure red and yellow, it can potentially look gaudy (not always a bad thing) as the three battle it out to secure our attention. But paler versions (shades) of the three colours in the form of pale pink, pale yellow and, you guessed it, pale blue are harmonious and somehow invite the accompaniment of grey. Richer versions of red, yellow and blue also sit well with a sumptuous, almost regal feel to their heavily saturated hues. The effects colours have on one another could fill a book and then another about how those colour associations change with differences in light, season and other nearby colours. Experimentation is key. No plant catalogue can compete with placing the real colours of actual plants beside one another in a nursery or garden.

Colour theory gives some great guiding principles but the colour wheel stops a long way short of showing every colour grouping or pairing possibility. Grey, for example, in its many shades looks smashing with oranges but the wheel doesn't highlight this. Equally, the right orange and pink can make for a striking pairing that the wheel also fails to note. Use it as a guide to build confidence but don't slavishly follow its rigid rules; try things out, pair plants at the nursery, be daring. I can often be found wandering around with cut flower stems and leaves, tentatively offering them up to potential partners like an eager matchmaker. This, more than anything, informs the way I put colours together.

Top **Unlikely pairings such as orange and grey can be surprisingly successful.**

Bottom **Few blues in nature are true. This campanula, like many so called blue flowers, carries hints of pink and mauve.**

HOW COLOUR AFFECTS US

Colour in the garden can have a profound effect on those in it. Mood, direction of movement and sense of space can all be manipulated with the careful placement and combinations of colour. Our eyes perceive colour in a particular way when viewing a large landscape or scene. Colours close up appear intense, often saturated and bright, but colours further from the viewer become less saturated and dulled. This is due to the limitations of our eyes, the light and atmospheric particulates. Artists use this technique to add depth to paintings and it can be used in the garden, too. Pale blues, greens, yellows and violets recess into the landscape and can appear further away than they really are. Conversely, bold reds, oranges and yellows jump out and appear closer. By placing 'bolds' close to the viewer and 'pales' in the distance it is possible to create an artificial sense of depth and space. It's also possible to direct the eye – and the foot – with the use of colour. Evergreen yellow plants dotted through a garden cause the eye to dart between the colour blocks in a zig-zag manner, adding to the overall sense of space. This technique works for movement, too, as the yellow draws viewers to it and therefore through the garden.

Mood is also malleable. Numerous studies on the effects of colour on our mental state draw similar conclusions. Red elevates our heart rate, therefore heightening our senses. This is perhaps the reason why drawing rooms were historically often painted red. Orange, according to a European study, stimulates intellect. Pale tones of blue and green are thought to calm and slow the heart, while bright yellows lift the spirits. This is, of course, all highly variable depending on colour perception (which is different for everyone), culture, origin, faith and life experience. The wider landscape, too, can be drawn into mood-altering colour compositions. By adopting the Japanese idea of Shakkei (meaning borrowed landscape), it's possible to repeat and draw in colours from surrounding gardens. This effectively increases the apparent size of a garden by visually borrowing neighbour's trees and the like and repeating their colours in our own garden. However you choose to 'use' colour to affect the garden, one thing is certain: more than form, texture or repetition, colour has the capacity to define the *genius loci* or spirit of place in a garden.

Top Repeated colours can lead your eye and ultimately your feet through the garden.

Bottom **Our** perception of depth and space can be altered to great advantage by carefully placing colour. Though growing together the red poppy appears closer to us while the blue cornflowers recess.

 Pale tones of blue and green calm and slow the heart, while bright yellows can lift the spirits. 〞

The dramatic yellows and pinks of this scheme can be easily identified and matched using colour charts.

DESCRIBING *and* IDENTIFYING COLOUR

Describing colour is a difficult matter. One person's lime green is another person's yellow-green, so a number of absolute colour systems exist across different industries involved with colour. Printers and designers often rely on the Pantone® colour system, consisting of thousands of colours each with an allocated international code and easily viewable on printed colour swatches. Scientists prefer the Munsell System for its precision, as it encompasses an impossibly large range of hues, tones, tints and shades laid out in complex swatches. For us gardeners there is the RHS/Flower Council of Holland colour charts. Clearly not every gardener is going to go out and buy colour charts, but for the purpose of this book I have referenced every colour to the chart's simple terms, opting for dark pink-violet, for example, rather than mauve, which is arguably more open to interpretation.

Colour is such a joy to experiment with and thanks to the unique qualities of plants it is an ever-changing challenge as season, light, weather and other plants all effect the colour of the species you choose and combine. The possibilities are endless.

ACHIEVING
YEAR-ROUND COLOUR

The 365-day garden relies on plants from every corner of the globe to ensure its colour longevity. Floral regions of the world burst into bloom year-round, so by selecting the best of the plants from these areas we are able to have colour every month of the year. Spring and summer are not such a challenge but when it comes to winter we often turn to plants from the southern hemisphere countries of Chile, Australia, South Africa and New Zealand which are naturally flowering then, as it's summer in their neck of the woods.

Not only do we rely on 'off-season' flowering to furnish the 365-day garden but also on plants capable of churning out flowers for months on end. The longest-flowering plants (see page 116) are irrepressible flower-factories for a number of different reasons. Some, through breeding, become sterile and unable to set seed, which is why plants such as *Geranium* Rozanne and *Geum* 'Totally Tangerine' (right) flower for months on end in a fruitless attempt to reproduce. Other long-flowering plants are selected from the wild or cultivated stock when a particular individual demonstrates a lengthier flowering season than its brethren. Human intervention in crossing and pollinating plants plays its part, too. Certain long-flowering plants, such as F1 hybrids, are effectively man-made. F1 hybrid seeds result from hand-crossing two parent plants with particular qualities. These may be colour, vigour or disease resistance but yield (flowers) is often highest up the breeder's agenda. This means that in most instances F1 hybrids will flower heavily over protracted periods due to good parentage. Outside of human intervention certain plants have naturally evolved to flower over long periods. Some plants grow in extreme environments with limited pollinators so to ensure success they flower for as long as possible. Others may have low germination rates and therefore need to produce a plethora of seed to ensure survival. Whatever their reason for long-flowering, these plants are invaluable in our 365-day gardens.

A SUCCESSION *of* COLOUR

Developing a 365-day garden needn't be an overly complex process. A few key plants can provide year-round colour, but to create a more dynamic garden calls for successional planting. By adding 'follow-on' plants, that can grow with, through, over, under or beside other plants that have passed their seasonal peak, we can ensure the maximum long-term colour per square metre. Certain groups of plants work well as 'follow-ons' to the rest of the garden's flora. Early bulbs that come and go before the garden has even woken up for spring, such as galanthus and eranthis, are perfect for planting under and around

deciduous shrubs and trees. A matter of weeks after leaf fall these diminutive plants follow on from the shrubs, bringing light and colour to otherwise bare earth.

As spring progresses and perennial plants emerge in a palette of various greens, further bulbs, such as tulips and alliums, are perfect among them. They will bloom right up to the point that the perennials come into colour, at which point they disappear. Later-flowering bulbs which bloom in mid- and late summer are also a boon. Planted through early summer perennials, the likes of *Galtonia candicans* and *Gladiolus murielae*

Multi-layered plantings featuring species which appear and disappear as the seasons change form the back bone of a good year-round garden.

Forget-me-nots scatter their seed far and wide. When a gap of soil and a chink of light appears, so do they.

bring fresh 'follow-on' life to areas suffering summer burn out. Self-seeders can help guarantee a succession of colour, too. The likes of *Verbena bonariensis*, verbascum, onopordum and forget-me-nots scatter their seed far and wide. These often lay around, just below the soil surface, awaiting their perfect moment. When a gap of soil and a chink of light appears, so do they. And these perfect follow-on plants can easily extend garden colour for several months through summer and autumn.

Another useful group of plants are the late-emergers. Species such as *Mirabilis jalapa* and *Asclepias syriaca* are perfect follow-on plants which can smother the senescing leaves and stems of long-since-spent spring perennials. Annual climbers are useful for succession, too. Ipomoea, cobaea and eccremocarpus will all rampage over tired shrubs or stocky perennials, taking follow-on colour well into autumn. Cannas and dahlias, pre-grown in pots and slotted into bare spots in summer, come into their own in autumn, too. Few plants can compete at this time of year with their sheer colour opulence.

Mixing successional or follow-on plants with other key players is a sure-fire way of getting extra colour into the garden without requiring lots of extra space. It's relatively easy to do and can help us take giant strides towards creating dynamic 365-day gardens.

Every plant featured in the seasonal chapters of this book has a suggested follow-on or successional plant which can be grown with it, to ensure maximum colour from every patch of the garden.

Self-seeders, annual climbers and late-flowerers keep the colour coming.

Clockwise from top left
Gladiolus murielae,
Onopordum acanthium,
Eccremocarpus scaber
and Mirabilis jalapa.

SPRING PLANTS

EARLY SPRING

Corydalis flexuosa
'China Blue'

There's something enchanting about this Chinese forest plant, with its lacy leaves and complex congestion of blue flowers that are almost too detailed to perceive individually. Grow it in dappled light in a humus-rich soil that doesn't sit wet in winter and it will thrive. Plant several together, if you can, below the canopies of mature deciduous shrubs somewhere close to a path edge (from where you can stare in wonder). A close relative of this corydalis is *C. lutea*; it's the yellow-flowered one that colonizes walls, cracks and crevices everywhere. I've welcomed it wherever I've gardened – it's resilient and can flower for nine months.

H/S 25cm × 30cm
Season of colour: Fls: spring; Fol: spring, summer, autumn
Colour combination: pink/yellow/dark red
Grow it with: *Primula denticulata*
Follow-on plant: *Aquilegia vulgaris* 'Nivea'

Primula vulgaris

One of Britain's prettiest natives, this primula grows wild in meadows, woodland edges and hedgerows. Its light yellow flowers peer up from its crinkled apple-green leaves, defying the cold from early to late spring. Happiest on moisture-retentive but free-draining soil, it will hunker down and slowly colonise a suitable area over many years. Crosses between it and *P. veris* result in highly floriferous, beefy plants that can outshine either of their parents. Try growing *P. vulgaris* on the peripheries of deciduous shrubs, where they'll stand out in early spring but will appreciate the dappled shade of the shrub later in the year.

H/S 30cm × 30cm
Season of colour: Fls: spring; Fol: spring, summer, autumn
Colour combination: light blue/light green/pink/purple
Grow it with: *Primula denticulata*
Follow-on plant: *Aquilegia vulgaris* 'Nivea'

Humulus lupulus 'Aureus'

This twining perennial climber embodies the urgency of early spring as it surges out of the earth at breakneck speed, growing up to 50cm a week. I use it purely for its foliage colour, which can light up early plantings and strike a nearly too vibrant contrast with early blue and purple bulbs. Left to its own devices it uses its rasping, spiraling stems to get a purchase on anything nearby. Grow it, in a more managed way, up a beanpole wigwam, on a trellis or through a hefty spring-flowering shrub. My favourite support is a simple post in the ground bound with pea sticks or prunings, where the hops can easily rampage away up to 6 metres or more in a neat-ish column.

H/S 6m × 50–60cm (grown on a frame/post)
Season of colour: Fls: summer; Fol: spring, summer, autumn
Colour combination: violet/ orange/white/brown-orange
Grow it with: *Rosa* 'Summer Song'/*Tulipa* 'Spring Green'
Follow-on plant: *Clematis* 'Polish Spirit' (pruned to 15cm in spring with the hops)

Anemone blanda

This anemone, like several of its buttercup relatives, is notable for its distinctive stamens which look like cute cartoon eyelashes set against mid-blue flowers. Its gnarled tubers may not look too promising when planted, but once they're established in a well-drained woodsy soil they will re-emerge each spring, having slowly claimed more ground over the last season. They are well suited to pots, too. I've grown them layered with mid-season tulips when their flowering span lasts long before and after the tulip. Grown in sun or dappled shade they are worth a try, as is *A. coronaria*, a taller, larger-flowered plant which has arguably the richest of all the spring reds and blues.

H/S 20cm × 30–40cm
Season of colour: Fls: spring; Fol: spring, summer
Colour combination: pink/white/ light yellow/purple
Grow it with: *Tulipa* 'Pink Diamond'
Follow-on plant: *Convallaria majalis*

Nonea lutea

The Boraginaceae family of plants provide more than their share of spring flowers, with the likes of *Omphalodes* and *Pulmonaria* in their ranks, but *Nonea* is often overlooked. Forming a low, compact dome it flowers through spring until late in the season, bearing a butter-yellow flower from a purple-brown calyx. It self-seeds but never rampages and can be easily spotted by its coarse, warty leaves and edited out where required. It makes a perfect woodland edge plant which sets off bluebells and early geraniums a treat. Don't remove old plants until the seeds have ripened and dropped — or failing that, save seeds on removal and sow them in summer.

H/S 30cm × 40cm
Season of colour: Fls: spring; Fol: spring, early summer
Colour combination: white/light blue/light violet/dark purple-red
Grow it with: *Anemone blanda*
Follow-on plant: *Lilium martagon*

Chaenomeles × superba '**Pink Lady**'

Grown in a mixed border behind perennials or splayed out on a wall, this wiry shrub covers the early spring shift in terms of colour. Other stunning quinces, such as *C. x superba* 'Crimson and Gold' and the elegant white *C. speciosa* 'Nivalis' follow, but *C. x superba* 'Pink Lady' is usually the first to blossom. Despite their oriental exoticism these shrubs are tough, tolerant of most soils and will thrive in sun or dappled shade. Their fruits are edible when cooked or made into jam, but I'd rather stick to the subtle perfume of the true quince – *Cydonia oblonga.*

H/S 1.5m × 1.5m
Season of colour: Fls: spring; Fol: spring, summer, autumn
Colour combination: silver/white/light violet/light yellow-green
Grow it with: *Clematis alpina* 'Pamela Jackman'
Follow-on plant: *Rhodochiton atrosanguineus*

Chrysosplenium macrophyllum

This relatively unusual plant falls somewhere between a bergenia, a saxifraga and a giant snowflake. Terminal cymes, a bit like cow-parsley heads, hold its small pinky-white flowers, each with a ruff of pale apple-white bracts. These tones, coupled with the burgundy hues of the stems, make for an elegant pallete. It's not a great socialiser so it needs its own spot away from overly enthusiastic perennials. Grow it in shade but not pitch dark, as it needs a little light and energy for its wandering rhizomes to slowly spread. Foliage is not as dense as its cousin, the bergenia, but it does make for a bold statement year-round.

H/S 30cm × 1m+
Season of colour: Fls: spring; Fol: year-round
Colour combination: silver/white/light blue/light yellow
Grow it: on its own but backed by *Deschampsia cespitosa* 'Goldtau'
Follow-on plant: *Ajuga reptans* 'Tricolor'

Tulipa clusiana

Split into numerous types, the range of tulips available is wonderfully overwhelming but it is easy to think of them in two basic groups: those that are perennial and return each year, such as some of the 'Darwins', and those that serve as single-season bedding. *T. clusiana*, with its alternating dark pink and white candy-stripe petals, reliably reappears when grown on a free-draining soil. It's slim with grey-blue leaves and ever so elegant. For a single-season display, *T.* 'Showwinner' is useful. It's really early, true red, lasts for three or more weeks and makes great compost come late spring! It looks lovely mingling with early dark violet crocuses.

H/S 30cm × 10cm
Season of colour: Fls: spring; Fol: spring
Colour combination: light violet/light pink/light blue
Grow it with: *Myosotis* 'Blue Ball'
Follow-on plant: *Allium cristophii*

10 MORE EARLY SPRING PLANTS

1. *Aurinia saxatilis*

2. *Brunnera macrophylla* 'Jack Frost'

3. *Viola odorata*

4. *Muscari comosum*

5. *Prunus cerasifera*

6. *Corylopsis pauciflora*

7. *Viola × wittrockiana*

8. *Sarcococca hookeriana* var. *digyna*

9. *Daphne mezereum*

10. *Hebe sp.*

Euphorbia polychroma

The chartreuse-coloured heads of this tightly domed euphorbia can befriend virtually any rich spring flower and quickly elevate its vibrancy, but beware pairing it with some paler tones. Powder pinks and washed-out yellows can look quite unsavoury in its presence. Grown on a free-draining soil with some air movement around it and no lanky perennials lolloping into its 'personal space', it will thrive. Try dotting it through border fronts or in a gravel garden. Think twice about the plants that will surround it as spring fades. Its own tones dull to a dirty mustard, suited to pairing with orange and red flowers or dark foliage plants.

H/S 45cm × 45cm
Season of colour: Fls: spring; Fol: spring, summer, autumn
Colour combination: violet,/orange/white/dark pink/red
Grow it with: *Tulipa* 'Princess Irene'
Follow-on plant: *Geum* 'Mrs J. Bradshaw'

Lathyrus vernus

Some pea relatives can demand a little TLC, but this early, clump-forming perennial vetchling looks after itself. I first spotted it in the garden of the late plantswoman and writer Margery Fish. It was merrily doing its spring thing while other perennials began their emergence. The flowers carry many tones of violet, purple, red and blue diffusing into one another and creating a delicious polychromatic haze. The plant reaches little more than 35cm high, which is possibly why Mrs Fish had it growing in rock banks and elevated areas where the viewer comes nearly eye-to-eye with the colour offerings. It's really not overly fussy and will flower well in dappled light on a humus-rich, free-draining soil.

H/S 35cm × 45cm
Season of colour: Fls: spring; Fol: spring, summer, autumn
Colour combination: light yellow/yellow-green/pink-purple
Grow it with: *Primula vulgaris*
Follow-on plant: *Allium caeruleum*

MID-SPRING

Smyrnium perfoliatum

This spurge-looking biennial is the ultimate flatterer of other spring plants. Bestowed with acid yellow-green bracts it gives an extra visual boost to spring species of virtually any colour. It quickly settles into part-shaded borders and woodland plantings, requiring little more than an annual edit to keep its self-seeding ways in check. I recall seeing it used somewhere in perfect combination with the orange-flowered *Berberis darwinii* and cinnamon-barked *Acer griseum* – very choice. Sow it in summer in shallow drills, keeping it moist until the seedlings have established – you'll never need to sow it again.

H/S 1m × 50cm
Season of colour: Fls: spring; Fol: spring
Colour combination: violet/purple/blue/orange
Grow it with: *Tulipa* 'Negrita'
Follow-on plant: *Lilium henryi*

Myosotis sylvatica

Once established in a garden this biennial or semi-perennial self-seeder is a perfect gap filler, popping up in areas of open soil or gravel. I have planted compact cultivar versions a few times as bedding but prefer to establish a few strategic plants of the true blue wild species and let it do its own thing. Flowering for 3–4 months from spring to summer, its habit is determined by environment – in the shade it extends long floaty flower heads, in the sun it's more compact and clump-forming. Its species name refers to its natural woodland habitat, with dappled shade and woodsy soil, but it's a chancer and will establish just about anywhere.

H/S 40cm × 30cm
Season of colour: Fls: spring, summer; Fol: spring, summer
Colour combination: light yellow/orange/light pink/white/purple
Grow it with: *Tulipa* 'Carnaval de Nice'
Follow-on plant: *Alchemilla mollis*

Lamium orvala

This is perhaps the best of the deadnettles. Orchid-looking flowers appear in its leaf axils in early spring but are a bit hidden until later on, when the plant has pushed up to 40cm. Borne in rings, the hooded flowers are very large for a nettle, with dirty pink tones and a speckled throat. They last well into summer. It makes a compact clump and does not ramble around like its fellow nettles. Grown on a free-draining but woodsy soil it will thrive, even dealing with low levels of dry shade. It's quite sociable, mixing well with various ferns and looks a treat with dark purple-brown tulips such as *Tuplia* 'Queen of Night'.

H/S 40cm x 40cm
Season of colour: Fls: spring, summer; Fol: spring, summer
Colour combination: dark purple-brown/purple/yellow-green
Grow it with: *Tulipa* 'Queen of Night'
Follow-on plant: *Lunaria rediviva*

Myrrhis odorata

Sweet cicely has been used for centuries as a medicinal herb. Every part of it is edible and can be used to add extra aniseedy sweetness to boiled fruit. Some books suggest it reaches 2 metres in a season, but in dappled shade I've seen it achieve little more than 1 metre. It flowers for several months through spring and into summer, producing wide umbels of dainty white flowers. Crop it to the ground in early summer and it will generate a fresh mound of its soft, strokable foliage, which will last till autumn. Grow it as the backdrop to a spring planting or in wilder areas in any moderate soil.

H/S 1m x 1m
Season of colour: Fls: spring, summer; Fol: spring, summer, autumn
Colour combination: dark green/purple/pale blue/pale pink/white
Grow it with: *Viola* 'Belmont Blue'
Follow-on plant: *Polemonium* 'Blue Pearl'

Malus 'Royalty'

There's no shortage of light pink spring-flowering trees, so the purple foliage and flowers of M. 'Royalty' provide a little dark relief. Purple paired with slightly darker purple should not work – but it does. This, coupled with a neat bun-shaped canopy and good vigour, is probably the reason I've loved it since I first encountered it as a teenager working in a nursery. It's a relatively small tree, reaching only 4–5 metres, but for smaller gardens M. 'Royal Beauty' has similar qualities and weeps at around 2 metres. You can grow either tree in virtually any garden soil in full sun to maintain the leaf colour. Staking low at planting time will allow the canopy some movement and aid root establishment.

H/S 6m × 4m
Season of colour: Fls: spring; Fol: spring, summer, autumn
Colour combination: light blue/red/light pink-purple/white
Grow it with: *Lunaria annua* 'Munstead Purple'
Follow-on plant: *Clematis* 'Purpurea Plena Elegans'

Fritillaria imperialis
'Kaiser'

Crown imperials, as they are known, are the biggest and most dramatic of the fritillaries. Their spring arrival is announced, even before they emerge from the soil, with an odd foxy smell emanating from their bulbs. Once above ground they take little more than four weeks to reach flowering point, when they produce a ring of bright orange flowers topped with a leafy mohican. Best grown in full sun on a free-draining soil, they are well suited to large rock gardens or dotted through a spring planting of ground-huggers such as hostas or lower-flowering bulbs. They don't usually require staking but benefit from some mollusc management.

H/S 1.2m × 30cm
Season of colour: Fls: spring; Fol: spring, summer
Colour combination: violet/purple/light yellow/green/blue
Grow it with: *Tulipa* 'Negrita'
Follow-on plant: *Allium hollandicum*

Viola
'Jackanapes'

There is something joyous about the hundreds of eager-faced flowers that this perennial bi-colour viola produces. With its upper two petals in dark purple-brown and the lower three in strong yellow it can be a challenge to place, but this variety works well with bronze- or yellow-leaved plants. Named, somewhat bizarrely, after the plantswoman Gertrude Jekyll's pet monkey, V. 'Jackanapes' will flower for three months or more. Grown in most soils in sun or part-shade, it will return each season – but it's worth taking cuttings to keep the plant fresh. Other violas, such as *V. tricolor* (violet, yellow and white) and *V. cornuta* (blues and whites) are good floriferous, long-term plants, too.

H/S 30cm × 25cm
Season of colour: Fls: spring–summer; Fol: spring, summer
Colour combination: yellow/dark purple-brown/yellow-green
Grow it with: *Euphorbia amygdaloides* 'Purpurea'
Follow-on plant: *Lysimachia ciliata* 'Firecracker'

Clematis
'Broughton Star'

There are many cultivars of *C. montana* that make fine garden plants. Flowering from mid-spring till summer, *C.* 'Broughton Star' quickly climbs walls, trellis or larger shrubs, adorning them with its scented, double, multi-tonal, purple-pink flowers. Planting the climber a few inches deeper than usual will reduce the chance of the dreaded clematis wilt. Pruning is usually restricted to removing dead, diseased and damaged stems, but I've given aged feral plants 50 per cent reductions which they've seemed to take in their stride. At 8 metres tall they need space to rampage, so pick a mature tree or shrub as support or run stems along the top of a trellis. A spot in full sun with moisture-retentive soil is ideal.

H/S 6m × 3m
Season of colour: Fls: spring, summer; Fol: spring, summer
Colour combination: dark pink/ yellow-green/light blue/silver
Grow it with: *Elaeagnus* 'Quicksilver'
Follow-on plant: Rosa 'American Pillar' (Rambler)

Dicentra formosa
'Bacchanal'

The common or garden bleeding heart is a reliable spring perennial but *D.* 'Bacchanal' has something extra. From a ground-hugging blanket of feathery, light grey-green leaves emerge its crimson-purple flowers. These heart-shaped blooms wobble in the breeze some 20cm above the foliage, forming a second layer of colour. The union of these flowers above grey-green foliage is, to my mind, one of nature's perfect pairings. Grow it in sun or part-shade so long as the soil is moisture-retentive. This plant is a perfect border-fronter, as after the flowers fade in early summer the foliage remains fresh for some months. Split it in spring when required.

H/S 40cm × 45cm
Season of colour: Fls: spring, summer; Fol: spring, summer
Colour combination: violet/pale blue/white/pink
Grow it with: Myosotis sylvatica
Follow-on plant: Tricyrtis 'Empress'

10
MORE MID-SPRING PLANTS

1. *Mertensia virginica*
2. *Epimedium sp.*
3. *Convallaria majalis* 'Albostriata'
4. *Lunaria rediviva*
5. *Geranium phaeum* 'Samobor'
6. *Clianthus puniceus*
7. *Phlox divaricata* 'Clouds of Perfume'
8. *Euphorbia amygdaloides* 'Purpurea'
9. *Aubrietia sp.*
10. *Akebia quinata*

Stylophorum lasiocarpum

This underused perennial is a
close cousin of the sun-
worshipping field poppy, but it's
most at home in dappled shade.
By late spring it's in full bloom
but it can produce its first yellow
flowers in early spring. Its
compact mounds of foliage make
for super groundcover planting
and the light green foliage
remains in good health till
autumn. It self-seeds in part-
shade but doesn't become
unmanageable. Planted through
an area of early spring bulbs
such as galanthus, its emerging
leaves will hide the sins of the
departing snowdrops as they
wither. Split in autumn or spring
and gather seeds for sowing
elsewhere in late summer.

H/S 50cm × 40cm
Season of colour: Fls: spring,
summer; Fol: spring, summer,
autumn
Colour combination: violet/pale
blue/orange/red
Grow it with: *Epimedium* ×
rubrum
Follow-on plant: *Crocus sativus*

LATE SPRING

Narcissus poeticus var. *recurvus*

This is truly a special daffodil. It's the last of the clan to emerge in very late spring and carries a sweet, quite unexpected jasmine scent which is refined and used in perfumery. Its flowers hold up nearly square to the horizon, displaying their clean white blooms which are centred with a compact corona in yellow with a red trim. Thought to have been one of the first narcissus to be cultivated, it may have played a part in the Greek legend of Narcissus. It is best grown in open areas with full sun and a moisture-retentive but free-draining soil. Place it close to a path edge for easy sniffing and picking.

H/S 45cm × 10cm
Season of colour: Fls: spring, summer; Fol: spring, summer
Colour combination: orange-yellow/violet/light blue/yellow-green
Grow it with: *Spiraea japonica* 'Goldflame' or on its own in turf
Follow-on plant: *Allium sphaerocephalon* (in the border)

Centranthus ruber

Thought of by some as a weed, this long-flowering perennial always has a place in my garden. Ok, it can be a bit forward in its colonising habits, but nothing that a hoe can't put pay to. If you get really lucky it might take a liking to your walls – which is better than a wayward buddleja. Flowers are on the washed-out side of red but sit next to most other colours with ease. Grow it in full sun on a low-nutrient free-draining soil. It's suited to wilder plantings but looks good dotted or self-sown through perennials. Crop it hard after the first flowering for a second flush or leave it to seed if you seek colonisation.

H/S 70cm × 50cm
Season of colour: Fls: spring, summer, autumn; Fol: year-round (just)
Colour combination: violet/light pink/green/dirty white/silver
Grow it with: *Lavandula angustifolia* 'Hidcote'
Follow-on plant: *Erigeron karvinskianus* (blooms while the centranthus rests)

Astrantia
'Roma'

From late spring till late autumn this delicate-looking perennial musters a succession of flowers, with a little break during midsummer. Each bloom rests on a fine stem and forms a cluster of mid-pink flowers backed by a paler 'ruff', which illuminates them. Though this useful perennial has only come back into fashion relatively recently, spurring a slew of breeding work, it has been grown as a garden plant for hundreds of years, gathering some appealing common names on the way, such a Hattie's Pincushion. Astrantias need an enriched moisture-retentive soil in full sun (or light shade) to thrive. Make the most of their weed-smothering foliage by splitting and expanding the colony every few years in spring. Deadheading pays dividends for a constant display.

H/S 60cm x 40cm
Season of colour: Fls: spring, summer, autumn; Fol: spring–autumn
Colour combination: violet/dark pink/light green/white/silver/blue
Grow it with: *Campanula glomerata* 'Superba'
Follow-on plant: *Allium* sp.

Iris sibirica

Unlike several other iris species, beardless *I. sibirica* continues to look good after its flowers have faded, thanks to its neat, columnar set of fine leaves. Grown in a moisture-retentive soil in full sun or very light shade it will flower for around four weeks each year. Flower stems hover over the foliage, each carrying three to five shapely blooms. It has spawned a rich spectrum of blue-hued cultivars such as the glorious *I.* 'Silver Edge'. The petals of this cultivar are framed with a white line, meaning their silhouettes are well shown off against one another rather than becoming an amorphous blob.

H/S 1.2m × 50cm
Season of colour: Fls: spring, summer; Fol: spring, summer, autumn
Colour combination: silver/light yellow/orange/white
Grow it with: *Geum* 'Totally Tangerine'
Follow-on plant: *Ligularia* 'The Rocket'

Polemonium 'Northern Lights'

The wild species of polemonium from which this plant arose manages two to three months of flower, but because *P.* 'Northern Lights' is sterile it flowers that little bit longer, stretching to over four months. When I first encountered it I feared that its squat habit was only selected by breeders so that more could be packed onto a shelved Danish trolley for transport, but this is not the case. Its diminutive habit is one of its strengths, along with very open flowers and the slightest wisp of a scent. Blooms are a bright light blue set of beautifully by the ferny hummock of foliage. *P.* 'Sonia's Bluebell', an even paler, yet vibrant blue-flowered form, is equally long flowering. Grow both in a free-draining but moisture-retentive soil in dappled shade.

H/S 30cm × 30cm
Season of colour: Fls: spring, summer; Fol: spring, summer, autumn
Colour combination: silver/light yellow/orange/white/purple/red/pink
Grow it with: *Astrantia major* 'Rubra'
Follow-on plant: *Nigella damascena*

Lupinus
'Terracotta'

The colour range of lupins was already huge, but thanks to dedicated breeding work their brethren is now bolstered with a new set of multi-tonal colours. What has been added to these soaring spires of colour is subtlety. Flowering for around six weeks in late spring and early summer, they are also blessed with mid-green palmate foliage which forms a pleasing mound and is often decorated with 'jewels' of rain or dew. *L.* 'Terracotta' combines light yellow, apricot and orange to form a multi-tonal optical mix of a light terracotta hue. Grow lupins in full sun on moisture-retentive but free-draining soil and site them away from the border edge, so that as their foliage fades later in the year it is hidden by other plants.

H/S 1m × 60cm
Season of colour: Fls: spring, summer; Fol: spring, summer, autumn
Colour combination: silver/light yellow/violet/blue/yellow green
Grow it with: *Iris sibirica*
Follow-on plant: *Nicotiana × sanderae* 'Domino Salmon Pink'

Aguilegia vulgaris var. stellata
'Ruby Port'

This classy aquilegia rose to fame as the star of Chelsea Flower Show a few years back. It seemed to appear in virtually every garden, which is no surprise given its uniform columnar nature and bevy of dark purple-red-coloured blooms. Like most of the genus, this plant thrives in dappled shade through to sun so long as it is on a reasonably moisture-retentive soil. It flowers for up to two months and shines among tall grasses, provided they are columnar, such as the slightly purple-burnished *Calamagrostis × acutiflora* 'Karl Foerster'. It is at home in herbaceous plantings or dotted around the edge of woodland. A shear over to ground level after flowering will rejuvenate the foliage.

H/S 80cm × 40cm
Season of colour: Fls: spring, summer; Fol: spring, summer, autumn
Colour combination: blue/light orange/light yellow-green/green-blue
Grow it with: *Euphorbia amygdaloides* var. *robbiae*
Follow-on plant: *Calamagrostis × acutiflora* 'Karl Foerster'

Campanula glomerata
'Caroline'

A confluence of light blue, white, violet and purple gives the dome-headed flowers of this reliable campanula an ethereal feel. Unlike some of its brethren, which are nearly too dark to see, this campanula sparkles in sun or part-shade, where it slowly spreads to form a useful, floriferous groundcover. Shearing off the first flush of flowers, as they fade, can sometimes trigger a second flush of blooms, taking colour all the way to late summer. Grow it at the front of mixed or herbaceous plantings with wispy grasses, darker violet blooms and silver foliage.

H/S 40cm × 60cm
Season of colour: Fls: spring, summer; Fol: spring, summer, autumn
Colour combination: purple/white/light orange/violet
Grow it with: *Aquilegia vulgaris* var. *stellata* 'Ruby Port'
Follow-on plant: *Salvia greggii* 'Navajo Dark Purple'

10
MORE LATE SPRING PLANTS

1. *Angelica archangelica*

2. *Olearia* × *scilloniensis*

3. *Abutilon* × *suntense*

4. *Hesperis matronalis*

5. *Glaucium flavum* f. *fulvum*

6. *Oenothera macrocarpa*

7. *Leptospermum scoparium* 'Red Damask'

8. *Gladiolus communis* subsp. *byzantinus*

9. *Calamagrostis* × *acutiflora* 'Karl Foerster'

10. *Nepeta racemosa* 'Walker's Low'

Geum rivale
'Leonard's Variety'

Squat plants can feel over-bred but this geum speaks of fairy tales and secret gardens. Flowering for around two months it produces blooms of a near unique red-pink with an orange-red flush set off by zesty light green leaves. The leaves form a compact hummock of attractive foliage once the plant has stopped flowering and can remain fresh-looking until winter. Grow several plants together to truly show off their special colour tones en masse, or use them as specimens in spring containers. Choose a site in full sun but ideally with a little afternoon shade. Splitting geums every few years in spring ensures good vigour and flowering.

H/S 40cm × 40cm
Season of colour: Fls: spring, summer; Fol: spring, summer, autumn
Colour combination: white/blue-grey/light violet/dark pink
Grow it with: *Lysimachia ephemerum*
Follow-on plant: *Alchemilla mollis*

GROWING
FOR COLOUR

GROWING *for* COLOUR

Colour rich displays can have their season extended, flowering increased and colour enhanced by applying a little horticultural knowhow.

Getting the most colour from a garden relies on more than picking and composing a well-selected palette of plants. Good establishment and carefully considered management is, of course, essential to ensure plants burgeon, bloom and fill the garden with colour through the seasons. Get a particular plant's position, soil, feeding, staking, mulching and watering right and it will establish well. Stay on top of pests and diseases and it will thrive. Apply some cunning horticultural techniques and it will prosper with more colour than ever.

Good establishment, maintenance and clever gardening can also encourage plants to flower more prolifically, earlier, later or longer. The delicious dark pink *Geranium psilostemon* is a case in point. Planted in full sun on well-prepared soil it will do ok, but an early and mid-season feed, followed by a savage trim after its first floral flush, will see it send up a second crop of foliage and blooms in late summer. Left to its own devices the geranium would only flower for a few months, but with a little garden know-how it keeps the colour coming for most of the growing season.

By starting with good basic gardening from the ground up and adopting a few easy horticultural techniques it's possible to establish and maintain a garden of kaleidoscopic colour 365 days a year.

UNDERSTAND *and* IMPROVE THE SOIL

Once you've gardened a plot for a few years you'll know all the foibles of the underlying soil – the corner that never dries out, the stony bit, the bit that nothing wants to grow in. But if you are new to a garden it is worth speeding up the process and having a dig around. A few old-fashioned profile pits (essentially a hole three spades deep) can reveal a surprising amount about the soil's structure, components, drainage and compaction.

It's also worth observing which plants are already growing in the garden as they may indicate its soil type and moisture-retentiveness. Some people get lucky and have the perfect rich dark brown topsoil which is free-draining yet moisture-retentive, but most gardens tend to veer towards too heavy or too light. Often these substrates can be planted to suit their natural moisture or nutrition level but most soils – be they sandy and light or clay and heavy – will benefit from the addition of organic matter. In both light and heavy soils it improves drainage, structure, microbial activity and nutrition. Organic matter can take the form of garden compost, composted green waste, mushroom compost, leaf mould or seaweed, but my personal preference is well-rotted farmyard manure. There was a time when this could be gathered for next to nothing but it's now a valuable commodity. An internet search will reveal a local supplier. I do the maths for how much I'll need like this: length of area to be improved × width × 15cm. This will give you the number of cubic metres you need to order. Delivery is in either 40-litre bags, one-ton dumpy bags or loose-tipped (if you have a big drive). When either single or double dug into the soil organic matter will make a huge difference to the plants you are trying to establish.

PLANTING

From the tiniest bedding plant to semi-mature trees, the basic planting method is similar. Every gardener has their own style and this is mine: Dig a planting hole at least twice the width and depth of the root ball of the plant you are installing. Mix organic matter (50/50) with soil from the hole and drop some of the mix back into the hole. Woody plants that have begun to spiral their roots around the inside of the pot need teasing out, perennial and annuals don't need this treatment. Settle the plant in so the top of its root ball is ½cm below the soil surface. Press the remaining soil in around the sides of the plant, ensuring good contact with the root ball. Don't press on the top of the root ball as this can split the roots lower down. Spread a fine layer of soil crumbs on top of the root ball and make a mini soil ridge around the plant with the remaining soil. Doing this prevents run-off when watering and directs the water down to the roots. Water plants in with 1 litre of water per litre of pot size – i.e., a 3 litre plant gets 3 litres of water. This serves to settle the soil, stabilise the plant and provide for its water needs in the first few days of establishment.

STAKING and SUPPORT

Plants in the wild get by perfectly well without gardeners needing to truss them up but garden plants and those taken from the wild into cultivation can need extra help. A wild plant gets a cushier life in the garden, with the potential of nutrient levels and water exceeding those in its natural habitat, which can lead to lush and potentially weak growth that needs supporting. 'Garden plants', as opposed to wild ones, have greater needs, too. Ever since humankind has cultivated garden plants we have selected, bred and hybridised to produce enhanced characteristics such as larger, heavier flowers. This means that some garden plants are now part disabled by our breeding and quite literally need support to hold themselves up. So, staking and supporting plants is a necessary evil and one which is, ideally, disguised so as not to detract from the appearance of the plant.

Right Early staking and support is essential for many lofty perennials.

Opposite left Growing perennials through a mesh of pea sticks supports the plants and reduces damage from heavy wind and rain while keeping flowering stems well place.

Opposite right A low stake, secured to new specimen trees and shrubs, can help aid establishment and prevent 'wind rock'.

Using pea sticks for support

The fine prunings of hazel and some other managed woodlanders are often known as 'pea sticks'. These fan-shaped twigs, usually around 1–1.5 metres long, have many side branches emerging from a central stem, meaning that once they're pushed into the soil the fanning branches can hold foliage and stems in place.

Like most forms of staking and support, timing is everything. Most staking work is ideally done in early to mid-spring before any significant foliage has emerged. This means the plants can subsequently grow through a structure and hide it in the process. Timing is also important for the pea sticks themselves. Once delivered in late winter or early spring, the sticks need storing in a shady place and are best used within a month or so. Leaving them longer than this sees the pea sticks become brittle and less amenable to the bending and twisting required to make structures. Pea sticks can be sourced from woodland managers and some private estates. It's also worth an online search and checking with your local visitor attraction garden for their source.

Structures for different plants

Herbaceous perennials and some annuals under 70cm are best supported by pea sticks pushed into the ground at 30cm intervals around each plant. This prevents them collapsing under their own weight later in the season, wards off wind damage and stops overly enthusiastic plants lolloping onto their neighbours.

EXAMPLE PLANTS

- *Knautia macedonica*
- *Gaillardia sp.*
- *Anthemis sp.*
- *Anchusa azurea*
- *Artemisia ludoviciana*
- *Aster × frikartii 'Mönch'*
- *Centaurea montana*
- *Rudbeckia var. sullivantii 'Goldsturm'* (to protect its neighbours)
- *Salvia verticillata 'Purple Rain'*
- *Scabiosa 'Butterfly Blue'*
- *Tricyrtis formosana*

Larger herbaceous perennials of 1.2 metres or more that can become top heavy or start to split at flowering time need a more rigid 'box' to support them. The technique involves pushing four stout bamboo canes into the soil in a square on the outer peripheries of each plant. Gaps between the canes are then filled in with pea sticks, which can be woven into each other as you proceed. Finally, tying a couple of string lines around the 'box' will provide extra strength. Especially long pea sticks can be folded over at the top and woven into their opposite number, so that extending plant stems are kept separated rather than forming a clump.

EXAMPLE PLANTS

- *Helianthus 'Lemon Queen'*
- *Rudbeckia laciniata 'Herbstsonne'*
- *Artemisia vulgaris*
- *Cephalaria gigantea*

Perennials that produce lofty flower spikes need a slightly different method of support. Pea sticks aren't up to the job here, but bamboo canes are ideal. Place them at the rear of extending flower spikes, so they're disguised, and use flexible twine to tie in the plants to avoid their expanding stems becoming strangled.

Link stakes are ideal as a replacement for pea sticks if you can't source them. They are usually coated in dark green plastic, which extends their life and increases their camouflage. Link them together in organic shapes as any perennials up to 1 metre begin to emerge.

Semi-mature shrubs and trees which are more than 1 metre high and liable to be rocked by the wind need hefty support from a timber stake in their first few years. A well-developed crown of foliage can create a significant 'sail' in high wind, potentially damaging roots, stems and the plant's chance of establishment. Use wooden stakes on the windward side of the plant, staking only around one third of the way up the trunk or stems. A flexible tie or adjustable belt is ideal here to prevent the plant from being strangled. For climbing plants see page 188.

EXAMPLE PLANTS

- *Delphinium* sp.
- Dahlias (support canes attached to key central stems)
- *Helianthus annuus*
- *Alcea rosea* (sometimes)
- *Verbascum* sp. (larger forms – sometimes)

EXAMPLE PLANTS

- Peonies
- Shorter delphiniums
- *Campanula lactiflora*
- *Phlox* sp.

EXAMPLE PLANTS

- Standardised trees – potted, bare-root or rootballed
- Semi-mature shrubs
- Semi-mature hedge plants (instant hedge)

WHAT and WHEN TO FEED

A new planting which has had its underlying soil prepared with well-rotted organic matter will not require feeding to the same extent as long-term established borders. Equally, any containerised plant grown in multipurpose compost will not need feeding immediately – most multipurpose composts have six weeks or so of food already in them. Containers filled with John Innes compost (a loam, sand and peat mix) will last even longer without the need for feeding – perhaps three months or more. Otherwise, general feeding of the garden is spread through the year, depending on the plant, though the lion's share is required in spring. This bolsters plants just as they are calling on water and nutrients to make their first tentative stems and leaves. It's vital to maintain feeding because as gardeners we often break the natural nutrient cycle by removing leaves and vegetation from the ground – one of the plant's nutrient sources in the wild.

The table (right) shows the feeding options for several plant groups – various mulching alternatives can be found on page 70. It's possible to meet a plant's nutritional needs organically, which is my preference, as long-term chemical usage effectively kills off natural organisms in the soil and affects its cycles and productivity. A worrying proportion of the world's agricultural land has been rendered useless as a result of chemical fertilisers.

PLANT TYPE	SEASON	FOOD	ALTERNATIVE
Established shrubs, trees, conifers, bamboo, etc.	Early spring	Balanced organic granular feed and mulch	Bone meal (slow-release and a good root boost)
Roses	Early spring	Manure mulch and granular fish, blood and bone	Garden compost, potassium-rich cocoa shells
Roses (and other greedy feeders such as dahlias and cannas)	Through summer	Liquid potassium-rich organic fertilisers (to boost flowering)	Potassium-rich seaweed meal
Herbaceous perennials	Mid-spring	Balanced organic granular feed and mulch	Fish, blood and bone (good for foliage and roots)
Herbaceous perennials	Early summer	Potassium-rich seaweed meal (for flowers and fruit)	Potassium-rich cocoa shells
Bulbs	Pre-flowering (can be at any time of year depending on the bulbs season)	Liquid seaweed fertiliser	Potassium-rich tomato feed (only use on container plants to avoid contaminating soil)
Bulbs	Post-flowering (for six weeks)	Liquid seaweed fertiliser	Potassium-rich tomato feed
Annuals	Summer – leading up to and through flowering period	Liquid potassium-rich organic fertilisers and compost added at planting time	Liquid seaweed fertiliser
Containerised plants	Early spring to mid-autumn	Liquid seaweed fertiliser	Liquid fertiliser with trace elements.

WATERING

We all know the benefits of watering when establishing plants but it's worth taking time to ensure that the plants are getting maximum benefit from your efforts.

✳ Create a mini soil ridge around newly planted specimens to 'focus' the water above the root zone and avoid run-off.

✳ Place a perforated pipe in the planting holes of larger trees or shrubs. Allow the end of the pipe to emerge above ground then simply top up with water direct to the root zone.

✳ Try to water only in the morning and evenings to avoid evaporation and leaf scorch.

✳ Avoid 'small and often' watering; this can lead to plants producing surface roots and becoming more susceptible to drought. Aim for longer, deeper waterings, but less frequently.

✳ Use rainwater where possible. It's more acidic than tap water and the plants will thank you for it. If it's a dry season and rainwater supply is scarce, fill water butts with mains water and leave it for 24 hours. This way the water will form carbolic acid on the surface and its pH will lower to become slightly more acidic.

✳ Aim to suit plants to their environment so that after the initial year of establishment watering they are able to fend for themselves.

✳ To save labour and make more efficient use of water, a perforated pipe irrigation system running under mulch can be highly effective and can be operated automatically from a timer on the tap. Peg the pipes down well as wily foxes often take a liking to the smell of rubber.

MULCHING

The benefits of mulching are many and various. Cloaking the earth in a rich blanket of good organic material adds nutrients, retains moisture, suppresses weeds, adds useful organisms and encourages worms and the like to drag this good stuff underground where it can aid root development. And it looks smart, too.

Well-rotted farmyard manure

Direct from the farmer this tends to be lumpy and coarse, which is not necessarily a problem, it just means you'll end up with a very thick mulch. It's suited to roses and other woody shrubs but herbaceous perennials benefit from the smaller particles of milled or crumbed manure. This is available bagged, in dumpy sacks or delivered as a loose load. Manure is rich in nitrogen and phosphate but low in potassium, meaning it will provide a good boost in spring to roots and shoots. It needs topping up annually.

Green waste

Making use of recycled waste in the garden is a no-brainer, however some recycling schemes are less than diligent about what ends up in the mix. Check that your local source of green waste is heat-treated and the only real issue you might encounter is variable nutrient levels and the occasional stowaway yoghurt pot!

Straw

A past lecturer of mine advocated straw as a mulch because it's cheap and easy to apply. I've only used it on outlying areas under large shrubs and trees in enclosed spaces where it can't blow around before it damps down and binds together. It provides low-level nutrition.

Bark/wood chips

Bark leaves a pleasantly finessed dark-coloured finish after it's applied and can last for many years without replenishment. On the downside, garden birds love to throw it around in pursuit of tasty insects and finer grades can drift off in the breeze. It's also the most expensive mulch. Wood chips can be cheaper but often have a dry, gnarled look once they've been down for a while. Both will release limited nutrients over time. If you are using chipped wood from a felled tree, leave it to mature for a year before applying it, as fresh chips can suck nitrogen out of the soil.

Gravel

Pea gravel or larger stones can work as an effective mulch but are best suited to rock and dry gardens. Elsewhere, gravel can get trodden in, makes new planting difficult and has no nutritional benefit – not to mention that is does look a little odd when surrounding lush herbaceous plants.

Membranes

I've experimented with planting through various membranes over the years, which are subsequently covered in something more attractive, such as bark chips. Success with this technique, in my experience, is limited to single trunk shrubs and the like. Clumping perennials and multi-stemmed shrubs end up lifting the membrane over time, which is less than pretty. A geotextile such as Terram® is ideal for this task. Initially it's a stark white but it quickly absorbs the colour of the underlying soil, thus disguising it.

> *Pea gravel or larger stones can work as an effective mulch but are best suited to rock and dry gardens.*

PESTS *and* DISEASES

Doing battle with a bevy of pests and diseases is a burden we gardeners must bear. While we strive for longevity of display, perfect blooms and 365 days of colour, so the bugs and blights attempt to live off our labours. Some are possible to ignore, others very specific and in need of niche treatments. Here are arguably the most common problems among establishing and mature plants and suggestions as to how to tackle them.

Pest and disease attacks weaken plants making them more susceptible to further attack and reducing their capacity to produce healthy leaves and flowers.

Powdery mildew

THE PROBLEM

This ailment is ugly above all else. A pale white-grey powder (the fungus) appears on leaves and stems eventually causing defoliation and a weakened plant which is more susceptible to attack from other pests.

THE SOLUTION

Powdery mildew tends to appear most commonly on plants enduring water stress. You can reduce the incidence of the problem with good watering (see page 69) and mulching. If the problem does occur, remove affected leaves. Fungicidal sprays are available if you choose to use them.

Scale insects

THE PROBLEM

These sneaky critters often look like little more than a series of small brown bumps on stems and the undersides of leaves. Underneath their shell (the bump) the insect plumbs into the plant, sucking sap and weakening it. The black mould that grows on the sap they excrete is often the first sign of their presence.

THE SOLUTION

Infections of this sap-sucker are often limited to single plants or parts of the plant, making it practical to physically remove them with your hands, a toothbrush or a swift blast of water from the garden hose. An organic fatty acid-based spray is also effective.

Rust

THE PROBLEM
Grouped together under the banner 'rust', this ailment is really a series of different fungi that thrive on live plant tissue. Yellow or brown spots or depressions on the leaf surface are an indication of the presence of orange/brown rust on the underside of the leaf.

THE SOLUTION
Rusts often occur in high humidity and transfer from plant to plant via splashes of water. Removing affected leaves can reduce the problem, along with increasing air flow if planting is particularly dense. Fungicidal sprays are also available.

Slugs and snails

THE PROBLEM
Molluscs and slugs are perhaps the greatest threat when trying to establish new plantings. A favoured fodder plant can be munched to the ground overnight. Slime trails and uneven chewing are indicators that the problem is slugs and snails rather than other leaf-chompers such as caterpillars and pigeons.

THE SOLUTION
To manage these little blighters effectively takes a multi-pronged approach. Watering on parasitic nematodes (microscopic worms) reduces slugs in the soil while copper bands and sheep daggings act as physical barriers. Part-plunged plastic cups filled with cheap beer lure some to a watery grave and hand picking (and squashing) in the evening, morning or after rain is effective, too. There is every chance that chemical pellets may affect other species, so I won't use them.

Aphids

THE PROBLEM
Appearing from late winter these winged sap-suckers in green, brown, red or grey are numerous and have a taste for newly emerged buds and leaves. A specialist once told me that the exponential reproduction of a single female's progeny through a season could equal 1 ton of aphids!

THE SOLUTION
Aphids are usually easy to spot on the growing points of everything from roses to delicate herbaceous plants. Hand squishing (if you can stomach it) is highly effective, along with water blasts from a garden hose or sprayer. Organic fatty acid-based sprays are also highly effective.

GARDENING TECHNIQUES
for MORE COLOUR...

Earlier, later and longer

By using a few simple horticultural techniques it's possible to enhance and increase the amount of colour a garden can produce year-round. And it doesn't have to be a huge horticultural hassle; a nip here, a tuck there and lots of plants are surprisingly amenable to flowering for longer, with more colour, before or after 'their season' – and some will even flower twice. Exhibitors at the RHS Chelsea Flower Show tinker with plants to get the perfect amount of blooms at the perfect moment. They manipulate growing and flowering cycles using sodium lights to create artificial 'mini days' in the middle of the night and often chill plants to hold them back. These professional growers work wonders but simpler ideas can deliver dramatic results at home, too. By accident and experiment, along with some sound advice, I've tried many means of getting more colour out of garden plants. Here are a few tried and tested techniques that work...

Extend the flowering season or trigger a second flush of flowers

One of the easiest ways of ensuring a continuity of colour is diligent deadheading, which can be a pleasure or a chore, depending on how busy you are. Seed heads which aren't left as bird food or ornament are nearly always best removed to prevent plants wasting energy on producing seed, but more importantly it can extend flowering by more than a month or trigger a second, later flush of flowers. This can work for lupins and delphiniums such as the delicious *Delphinium* 'Spindrift' (opposite).

The box (right) suggests a few plants that will bloom for longer with deadheading but it's not worth doing it to all and sundry. Popular perennials such as *Geranium* Rozanne, *Geum* 'Totally Tangerine' and *Erysimum* 'Bowles's Mauve' are sterile and incapable of making seed, therefore deadheading them is folly and quite unnecessary. They will continue to bloom irrespective of your efforts.

PLANTS TO DEADHEAD OR CUT BACK AFTER FLOWERING

- *Achillea* sp.
- *Alcea*
- *Anthemis tinctoria* 'E. C. Buxton' and sp.
- *Aquilegia* sp.
- *Astrantia major*
- *Centranthus ruber*
- *Centaurea montana*
- *Coreopsis* (larger flowered species)
- *Dianthus* sp.
- *Dicentra formosa*
- *Delphinium* sp.
- *Geranium psilostemon* (full cut back for second flowering)
- *Knautia macedonica* and *Cephalaria* sp.
- *Kniphofia*
- *Lavandula*
- *Leucanthemum*
- *Lupinus* (full cut back for second flowering)
- *Rosa*, some species
- *Salvia nemorosa* (full cut back for second flowering)
- *Scabiosa* sp.
- *Verbascum* sp.
- *Viola odorata*

Get biennials to flower twice

Biennial plants, which make a rosette of foliage in their first year and bloom in the second, usually die after they have flowered. This untimely death, after you've looked after them for two years, needn't be the case. *Digitalis, Dianthus barbatus, Hesperis* and *Alcea* can all be coaxed into flowering again. By removing flowering stems and preventing these plants from producing seeds there is a good chance that they will re-bloom. Sometimes it's during the same year, or they can re-flower in their third year. It takes minimal effort to remove the flowering stems of these plants and it often provides ample dividends.

Hone super-sized blooms

Though this technique is somewhat limited regarding the plants it can be applied to, it has dramatic effects. Perennials such as *Chrysanthemum* sp. and dahlias will produce bigger, more dramatic blooms if all their energy is focused on the apical tip where the leading bud is located. To do this simply involves removing lateral flower buds so the plant's energy is focused entirely on the leading flower bud. On the downside, this does often means that these larger blooms require staking.

Persuade plants to flower up to a month later than usual

A good proportion of herbaceous perennials flower during the seasonal peak of late spring and summer but some can be persuaded, by means of pruning, to bloom later in the year. Many of the daisies, phlox and veronica will flower a month later, on more compact plants, if they are reduced by around half their height in late spring. It's commonly referred to as the 'Chelsea Chop' because it should be carried out during the RHS Chelsea Flower Show week in late spring. Flowers are often smaller following a prune, but that is countered as plants are also endowed with more of them. The occasional one-off, such as *Aster* sp., should be pruned in midsummer but the bulk, as highlighted right, are sure-fire spring-prune winners. If you are an inexperienced Chelsea-chopper, try this technique with heleniums for guaranteed later flowering on more compact plants.

PLANTS TO 'CHELSEA CHOP'

- *Phlox paniculata*
- *Monarda sp.*
- *Aster sp.*
- *Echinacea purpurea*
- *Eupatorium sp.*
- *Gaura sp.*
- *Helenium sp.*
- *Sedum sp.*
- *Heliopsis sp.*
- *Lobelia cardinalis*
- *Rudbeckia sp. (perennials)*
- *Teucrium chamaedrys*
- *Tradescantia × andersoniana*
- *Veronica spicata*

Certain perennials will bloom later in the season, with more flowers, if they are cut back by around half in late spring.

Winter protection for earlier flowering

Exotic, colour-rich, high-drama plants such as *Echium pininana*, *Solanum crispum* and shrubby salvias can be coaxed into flowering earlier in the year with the help of protection over the winter. Grow them in a hot spot and provide extra protection; simple frames made from bamboo tied together with string or cable ties and wrapped in fleece work a treat. For plants such as *Echiums* that will suffer in the winter wet, add a plastic roof or hood.

Spring warm up for faster flowering

Warming up the soil prior to planting is not just the preserve of the vegetable gardener. An area due to be sown or planted with ornamentals will benefit from having a fleece or similar placed over it for a few weeks in advance of working the soil. This way, seeds will germinate faster and roots establish quicker – all leading to getting the colour kicked off sooner.

Earlier flowering from early sowing

Early sowing in a frost-free glasshouse or coldframe can have a number of benefits. Many perennials that usually take two years to flower from seed, such as *Gaura*, *Gaillardia*, *Pennisetum* and *Berlandiera*, can be persuaded to flower, albeit moderately, in their first year from an early spring sowing. And a number of annuals which originate from hotter climes, such as *Cleome* and *Laurentia*, must be sown early if they are to bulk up and flower in time for summer. Early flowering advantages can also be obtained by very early sowing of plants such as sweet peas. *Lathyrus* sp. can be sown in early to mid-winter in cold frames or a cool glasshouse, however, they can be a pain to maintain over winter and watering should only be in moderation. Come mid-spring they can be planted out (following some pinching to encourage side branching and more flowers) when they will flower some 2–3 weeks earlier than spring-sown plants.

Continuing colour with successional sowings

Due to extreme growing conditions in their natural habitat, many annual plants are hardwired to flower and set seed in a hurry. This guarantees survival, but as a colour-hunting gardener I want more from them. The flowering period of some annuals can be extended with deadheading but successional sowing is more successful with others. *Papaver somniferum*, which parades magnificent translucent blooms for a miserably short two weeks, can be successionally sown to bloom for six weeks or more. I've found the old-fashioned pot marigolds, *Calendula officinalis*, work well treated this way, too. Simply sow the seeds in mid-spring into scratched-out lines in a sunny piece of well-prepared soil. By the time you sow the second batch, three weeks later, the first ones will have emerged. Follow this up with a third sowing another three weeks later. Amazing weather can sometimes bring the three sets of flowering closer together, but you are guaranteed to have a longer flurry of flowers than a single sowing can muster.

Earlier colour from glasshouse growing

Glasshouse space is always at a premium in spring but if you can squeeze in a couple of extra plants try growing dahlias and cannas in 10-litre containers. Potted up in early spring and grown in the glasshouse, these exotic tender plants will flower up to a month earlier once they are transplanted to the garden in early summer. Slotting them into an establishing bed can be a challenge, so in early spring I often plunge empty 10-litre pots into the soil where I know the dahlias or cannas are destined to go. Come summer, the empty pots can be removed and the de-potted plants slotted into the hole left behind. Colour in an instant!

Instant colour off-the-shelf

At certain times of the year it's possible to buy plants that have already been manipulated for you. In autumn the pot-mums arrive in the garden centres, all pincushion-perfection with a dome of cheek-by-jowl daisies. These plants are not trimmed and topiarised; it's a horticultural chemical that shortens the gaps between their leaf nodes which leads to a manipulated, but colour-rich, plant. Make the most of them in their first year as when the chemical wears off they will return to their original lankier form and are often only fit for the compost heap.

> ❝ *In autumn the pot-mums arrive in the garden centres, all pincushion-perfection with a dome of cheek-by-jowl daisies.* ❞

Pruning and not pruning

There are plenty of good reasons to prune but occasionally it's fun to tear up the rule book and manage your plants just for colour. *Clematis* 'Perle d Azur' is a group 3 clematis, so it should be hard-pruned in late winter ready to create a fresh batch of stems in spring. Left to its own devices, however, it can flower earlier and its blooms will embellish a much larger plant. In other words, more colour. I wouldn't let the plant go a second year without a prune as it starts to become a bit feral and sparce, but one year on, one year off seems to work. This can be applied to several plants.

Cornus and salix make for great winter colour when hard-pruned in spring to ensure they continue to produce lots of colourful young basal stems. Cultivars such as *Cornus* 'Midwinter Fire' are not as vigorous as some, often only growing 40cm stems each year. Left to their own devices, rather than being pruned, they will reach 1m in two years and although their colour intensity reduces there is more colour overall.

Conventional wisdom suggests hard-pruning shrubby salvias (left) in spring; sometimes this is essential if they've become too ragged and moribund, but if you can get away with leaving them unpruned they will flower one to three months earlier in the garden. Of course, this technique only works for certain plants but it's worth trying it out here and there as a means of souping-up the colour of your existing planting.

Forcing for 'out-of-season' colour indoors

Forcing plants out of dormancy and into action is a practice that dates back centuries. Long before the first pineapple was persuaded to produce a fruit in murky Europe, growers had used combinations of heat and light to manipulate plant behaviour. Forcing rhubarb, the practice of getting the plant's stems to emerge and blanch without light, is an early example. Some claim the practice was 'discovered' at the Chelsea Physic Garden in London. For your own glasshouse or windowsill a few adventures in forcing are great fun and, most importantly, add to your ranks of colour. 'Prepared bulbs' of hyacinths and narcissus (usually chilled into thinking they've been through a winter) are designed for forcing. Most are available for planting from early autumn. Different bulbs need slightly different treatment, which is usually indicated on the pack.

Forcing hyacinths goes something like this:

1. Moisten bulb fibre and fill a shallow pot (around 15–20cm deep).

2. Plant the bulbs with their 'noses' just sticking out of the fibre.

3. Place the pot in a cool dark place ensuring the compost remains damp.

4. After two months bring them into daylight (not blazing sunshine).

5. In a matter of days the leaves will have greened and the flowers emerged.

Cornus stems can carry twice the amount of colour through winter if they are hard pruned every other year.

'Forced' bulbs can bring welcome colour to the home, conservatory, glasshouse or sheltered court yard in the depths of winter.

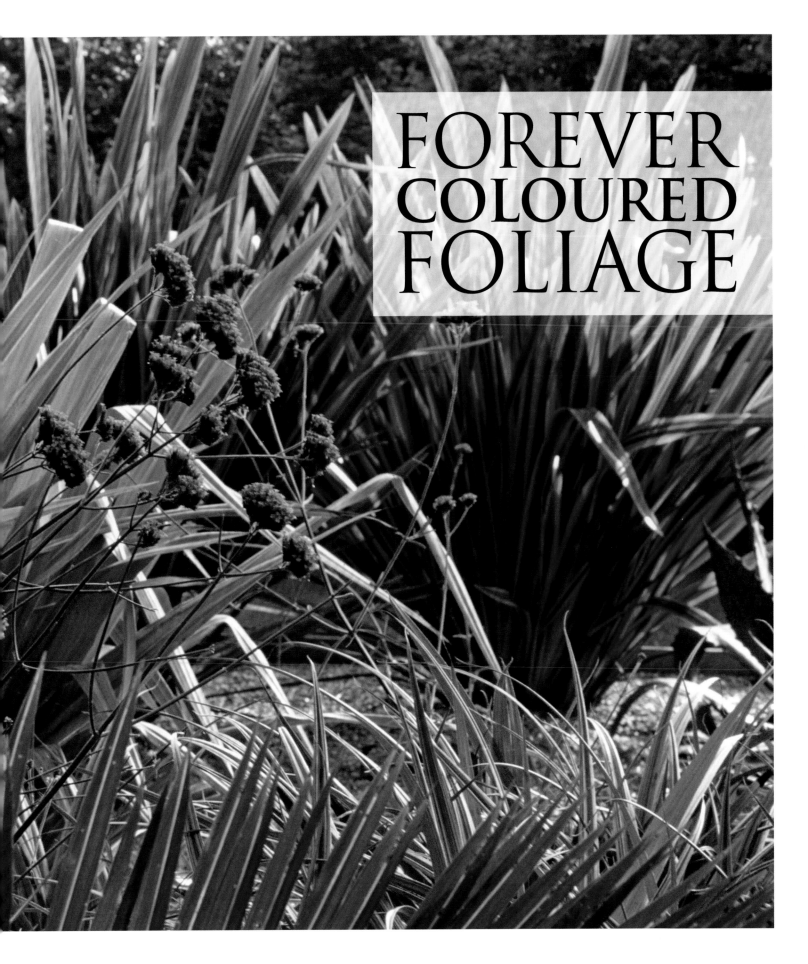

FOREVER COLOURED FOLIAGE

YEAR-ROUND FOLIAGE COLOUR

The most vital components in giving the garden 12 months of non-stop colour are those rugged, stick-it-out-in-all-weathers stalwarts; the sort of plants that retain a perky, colourful enthusiasm despite winter clouds and the weight of a stubbly hoar frost; the sort of plants that give the garden a structure and sense of life when the annuals and perennials fade; the sort of plants that have evergreen foliage but bring colour to the garden in other seasons, too. These special members of our horticultural palette are, of course, the irrepressible 365-day plants. A few of these year-rounders can produce flowers for twelve months (see Longest Flowering Plants on pages 116–125), but the majority rely on foliage and stems to keep up the colour every day of the year.

Colour-rich leaves

The range of hues year-round plants provide doesn't quite compete with summers palette but it is impressive none the less. From the inky emerald of evergreen shrubs, which often dominate gardens, through a vivid spectrum taking in yellows and oranges to light blue, grey, purple and red. Paired and placed in the right way, these year-rounders bring colour, form, texture and backdrop to other plants which rise, flower and fade around them. This quirky bunch of ferns, palms, shrubs, grasses and conifers provide the most vital element of any all-season garden – come rain, hail, snow or drought they still burn bright with colour.

Coniferous colour

Conifers may not have the glamorous allure of a willowy, fine-flowered perennial but their year-round, weatherproof needles guarantee colour, making them ideal 365-day plants. They're effective dotted through the garden repeating the same colour and form, or they can be used as statement plants or clipped into hedges and topiary. The colour range among conifers is wide, including virtually every green, endless blues, yellows, muddy reds and grey. With the year-round foliage of these trees creating potentially monolithic slabs of colour in the garden, it's worth considering their wider visual impact. Species with dark, oppressive green foliage such as *Taxus*

baccata – yew – have a light-absorbing, sombre hue and recess into the landscape, while too much pale blue from the likes of junipers can feel cold and distant. Bright yellow (often called gold for marketing purposes) can do the reverse and radiate eye-squinting colour out of the murk with too much vigour.

For this reason, it's worth carefully considering where to place year-round conifer colour and which hues to place it with in order to 'balance', lighten or darken the space. Some conifers have their own 'balance', with multi-tonal foliage that is neither too attention-grabbing nor recessive. *Thuja occidentalis* 'Rheingold' is one of these plants and one of the few 'yellows' that isn't too bright for winter. Its foliage may have mid-yellow as its base but it carries orange and pink tints on new growth and also in the cold. It has a bulbous conical form and potentially reaches 1.5 metres high, making it ideal for the border. Blue conifers are less attention-seeking than gold but to my mind are equally fresh in the right quantities. The shapely form and multi-tonal blue-grey hues of *Chamaecyparis pisifera* 'Boulevard' (8m x 4m) look good in every seasonal light from golden to grey. This plant was de rigeur when I worked in my first horticultural job as a teenager in the 1980s. Back then, it was strictly paired with heathers, which are now out of fashion, but its loose conical form, soft strokeable

Top The rich foliage of Taxus shows off brighter plants.

Bottom Thuja occidentalis 'Rheingold' carries colour year-round.

foliage and slight weep to its growing tips is as lovely as ever. The equally blue *Juniperus squamata* 'Blue Star' (0.5m × 1m) is a very different beast. It's a groundcover conifer and distinctly not strokeable, with sharp spiny needles forming a billowing cloud. Both these blue conifers, along with the huge *Cedrus atlantica* Glauca Group, retain consistent colour year-round. This tone works perfectly when paired with transient red flowers, leaves or berries.

When it comes to hedging conifers, rather than ornamental ones, I often opt for *Thuja plicata*. It is certainly not a showy plant but it works well as a hedge, especially when the glossy sheen of its foliage is picked out in winter light. It has a more uplifting green than yew, with hints of yellow, but not in a sickly way, and it makes a cracking hedge which is much more manageable than × Cuproyparis leylandii. Like yew, it can also be worked into clipped topiary forms.

For a more multi-tonal conifer, *Cryptomeria japonica* 'Vilmoriniana' (1m × 1m) is worth a try. This dwarf Japanese cedar often blushes with dirty purple and red hues through the coldest seasons, setting off beige grass stems a treat. Its cousin, the irregularly shaped, cloud-like *Cryptomeria japonica* 'Elegans Compacta' (3m × 1.5m), also carries an embarrassed, bronze-red hue in winter on foliage that has a soft spongy look to it.

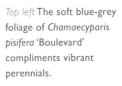

Top left The soft blue-grey foliage of *Chamaecyparis pisifera* 'Boulevard' compliments vibrant perennials.

Top right *Thuja plicata* forms a tight glossy hedge with none of the problems associated with × Cupressocyparis leylandii.

Bottom left Pale blue *Cedrus atlantica* Glauca Group becomes a huge tree but can be maintained as a hedge.

Bottom right *Cryptomeria japonica* 'Vilmoriniana' carries autumnal tones through much of the year, especially winter.

Functional or quirky, topiary brings year-round form and colour to the garden.

Topiary colour

Clipped geometric forms work brilliantly as transitional elements between built structures and planting but they're equally important for their year-round colour. Box and yew are the plants that traditionally receive this treatment, but they both have fairly uninspiring winter hues. Other evergreens with more vibrant foliage can be used in their place. *Lonicera nitida* 'Baggesen's Gold' works well for small-scale topiary endeavours , with its evergreen, light yellow leaves and dense branching habit. It will happily take tight pruning for a decade or more in forms as complex as you can imagine. Many of the pale-leaved *Pittosporums* also respond well to a clip and they're dense enough to form substantial 2 metre or higher topiary creations. For smaller shapes, *Pittosporum tenuifolium* 'Tom Thumb' can take clipping into cubes or balls. Its foliage is glossy and dark purple, meaning it needs a spot in full sun to stop it disappearing into the background.

Most of the evergreen *Euonymus* will also take to topiary. Their leaf size and habit means you'll never achieve total perfection, but for columns, balls and boxes they suffice. Cultivars with gold or white variegation tend to read most strongly. Several of the conifers, including *Thuja* and *Taxus* (the gold form is best), respond well to long-term topiary pruning, but for truly individual clipped colour try *Cedrus atlantica* Glauca Group. Hard-pruned from the outset, this usually huge tree can be persuaded to become a dense column, cube or pleached hedge of pale blue. A toparian triumph.

“ *Nandina domestica's skinny, elegant foliage will obligingly flutter in the slightest breeze, bringing much-needed animation to the garden.* ”

Forever-green shrubs

Broad-leafed evergreens can provide the lion's share of winter colour, but I tend to avoid blocky, dark-leaved plants such as plain *Euonymus fortunei* or *Sarcococca*, which can drift into the shadows and bring little to the garden. Shrubs such as *Acca sellowiana* and *Nandina domestica*, however, are near perfect 365-day plants. The underused *A. sellowiana* is a year-round delight, especially when it's pruned to maintain a compact form. Its leaves have a grey felting to their undersides which is only revealed when caught in a breeze. The flowers, when they arrive in summer, are complex and exotic with an explosion of red stamens held in hefty petals which are pink above and white below. A year-round star.

Many of the useful ever-coloured shrubs tend to be a little stiff and less interesting for their resistance to a breeze, but *Nandina domestica* is different. Its upright, columnar habit is similar to some bamboos and its skinny, elegant foliage will obligingly flutter in the slightest breeze, bringing much-needed animation to the garden in low season. This, coupled with red-tinted leaves through winter, panicles of white flowers in summer and autumn berries, make it one of the very best 365-day plants. Its close competitor,

with several seasons of interest and evergreen foliage, is *Arbutus unedo* 'Compacta'. This squat strawberry tree has desirable cinnamon-coloured branches, white urn-shaped flowers in autumn and marble-sized red-orange fruits which are most evident in late summer and early autumn. These are edible – just – but the Portuguese make a more palatable brandy from them.

Twelve months of varied interest can't be bad, but the strawberry tree is not the only choice evergreen that delivers the goods. *Ageratina ligustrina*, a South American native which used to be classified as a shrubby *Eupatorium*, is a 'must-have', too. Its loose corymbs (flattened heads) of white flowers dust the shrub with thousands of blooms in autumn. But it's the foliage that marks out this plant as special. Despite being a standard-issue dark green, the leaves are delicate and well-spaced, giving the shrub a light, partially see-through quality that is not present in most evergreens.

Larger-leaved year-rounders are worth a grow, too – if you have space to spare. Japanese plants step up to the mark here. Both *Fatsia japonica* and *Eriobotrya japonica* carry tough, exotic-looking leaves up to

30cm long through the worst of the winter weather. Fatsias have glossy, palm-shaped, mid-green foliage and bear their ivy-like flowers in winter. I use these 'look-at-me' shrubs with caution, pairing them with other year-rounders to avoid them looking alien in the winter landscape. Situation is vital, too. On poor soils or when buffeted by sharp winds these shrubs can become chlorotic with sick-looking yellow foliage and burned edges.

Several variegated cultivars of fatsia are lurking out there in nursery-land but few seem to have the vigour of their plain-green parents. *Eriobotrya japonica* is a very different plant which, despite its numerous qualities, falls into the unfortunate category of 'dark-leafed evergreen shrub'. Its saving grace is the sheer scale of its crinkly inky-green leaves. These are best shown off against the lighter, smaller foliage of bamboos and the like.

Finally, for near year-round perfection, *Luma apiculata* is hard to beat. This Chilean evergreen matures to become a small multi-stemmed tree with irresistible rusty-orange trunks. Add to this its spring/summer flowers and autumn berries and this might just be the ultimate 365-day evergreen.

Coloured evergreen
foliage shrubs such
as *Hebe* 'Silver Dollar'
and *Lophomyrtus*
(below) along with
Choisya ternata
'Sundance' (below,
right) guarantee
vibrancy whatever the
weather.

Forever-coloured shrubs

For zingy year-round foliage that can glow in the gloom, Australasia provides an array of plant options. New Zealand, which is home to many year-rounders, gives us hebes. These robust shrubs have a particular soft amenable quality in both foliage and flower that I find makes them easy to place amongst mixed plantings or even in herbaceous borders. *Hebe* 'Silver Dollar' is one such plant. It has a distinctive symmetry to its evenly spaced racks of leaves which are thick, rounded and broadly edged with cream. These look good year-round and are further enhanced by its long-season light violet flowers which appear between spring and autumn. A slightly sheltered site will keep it in good fettle or it works well in a container close to the house. Another hebe for the colour-hungry is *H.* 'Heartbreaker'. True, this plant does look like it's overdone it with the make-up, resulting in vivid-pink artificial-looking growing tips and extreme variegation elsewhere, but when all else fails this carnival of colour will sustain.

For a slightly more subtle injection of foliage colour, the oft overlooked *Lophomyrtus* × *ralphii* 'Magic Dragon' is lovely, despite its frivolous name. This compact shrub is adorned with small, ribbed, raindrop-shaped leaves on delicate wiry stems. Tone varies

from burgundy with a cream edge through to green and even pinks, giving a multi-tonal haze of colour. It can work as a low hedge, container specimen or mid-border shrub, where its colours can set off a succession of other plants nearby.

Australia is home to many ever-coloured plants, too, and none is more useful than eucalyptus. Often known as widow-makers in Australia, due to their propensity to drop large branches for no particular reason, they have been adopted around the world for timber, resin and ornament. The classic garden plant is *Eucalyptus gunnii*. Through the seasons this plant sustains its pale blue-grey foliage but I'd never let one grow to full size. Like its regional cousin *Acacia dealbata*, it can look very odd at full scale in an otherwise predominantly green landscape. I prefer to maintain it as a shrub with annual or biennial hard-prunes to keep it under 3 metres. This way it will also maintain its distinctive juvenile foliage. These young leaves wrap around the circumference of their stems creating round, or to be technical, perfoliate leaves. These leaves and stems are perfect for flower arranging, so much so that I've planted them in cutting gardens as their annual hack results in endless useful bouquet-fillers.

> 66 *For zingy year-round foliage that can glow in the gloom, Australasia provides an array of plant options.* 99

Top Heuchara 'Peach Flambe' glows in
even the greyest conditions.

Bottom Epimedium x rubrum
carries colourful foliage virtually
year-round.

Opposite, clockwise from top
Bergenia purpurascens often develops
rich autumnal tones in winter.
Cynara scolymus continues to produce
new leaves through winter.
Rumex sanguineus var. sanguineus
seeds freely under shrubs and trees.
Arum italicum 'Pictum' provides
welcome fresh foliage in winter.

Plants with rigid leaves or stronger stems can take a battering yet maintain a dignified look and lasting colour.

Perma-colour perennials

Some evergreen perennials can let the garden down through winter. After a summer of enthusiastic growth they can get that wet-dog-after-a-walk look – all damp and slumped in the corner. Pulmonarias and kniphofia tend to do this, but plants with rigid leaves or stronger stems can take a battering and still maintain a dignified look and lasting colour. Bergenias fit the bill here; they can tough it out and look lively through the coldest months, and glow with life and vigour given the assistance of backlight. *Bergenia purpurascens* has narrower leaves than some of the genus, but these perky mid-green paddles can be really showy as they glide through tones as rich and various as purple, orange and red. On a smaller scale, heucheras, with their compact bun of foliage and kaleidoscopic colour range, thanks to US breeding, keep the colour alive through autumn and winter. Some cultivars can adopt the slumped pooch look but *Heuchera* 'Peach Flambé' is a favourite of mine because it holds its colour, albeit not as bright as in summer, and sustains a perky habit. Heucheras look good when planted en masse or bubbling over the edge of tubby cauldron pots. Root-munching vine weevil larvae love them, though, so a treatment with predatory nematodes is necessary to ward off the bugs. They grow in full sun or part shade and are well partnered with *Epimedium x rubrum*. This colour-rich Japanese plant is, despite its papery thin leaves, able to last out the winter, often carrying its ruddy burnished tones through till spring. Try planting it as an understorey to woody winter evergreens such as *Mahonia*.

For super-sized silver foliage that continues to grow nearly year-round, the globe artichoke, *Cynara scolymus*, is great value. Rather than consign these bulky vegetables to the kitchen garden, I like to use them as ornamental foliage plants. They work well at the Chelsea Physic Garden in the herbaceous border; here they serve as a backdrop to winter bedding and a perfect foil to the annually changing displays of tulips, annuals and perennials around them. A split every few years stops them becoming monstrous.

Two other evergreen perennials deserve a mention, but I'd exercise caution in introducing them because both are self-seeders and can get quickly out of hand if left unchecked. *Arum italicum* 'Pictum' and *Rumex sanguineus* var. *sanguineus* carry weather-resistant foliage through autumn, winter and spring. *A. italicum* sits dormant through much of summer with only its green berries thrust above the soil on short stems, but come winter these fruits turn bright orange and its marbled green and white foliage emerges. Remove the berries before they drop or the birds will begin a redistribution programme. *Rumex sanguineus* var. *sanguineus* only tends to seed in its immediate vicinity so it's unlikely to become a significant problem, but in dry shade its propensity to proliferate might be seen as an advantage where little else dares to tread. Its foliage forms neat rosettes through the winter, hugging the earth with pointed, mid-green leaves shot through with striking purple-red veins.

Bright blades

Evergreen grasses and bamboos bring much to the 365-day garden, adding year-round freshness of colour and form without much effort. Stiff-leaved species such as *Yucca*, *Phormium* and *Cordyline* hold their colour and shape against rain and wind but can suffer if temperatures hold below -5 degrees. To preserve them it's worth being ready with the fleece if Arctic temperatures are forecast, but I avoid wrapping up for the duration of winter as these plants don't appreciate the humidity and then, of course, their colour is hidden.

Yucca filamentosa "Color Guard', like several of the cultivars mentioned here, is brash but when well paired it can work a treat. Its broad, yellow, central variegation and spiky explosion of blades is eye-catching every day of the year. This makes for a dramatic statement, but for a more balanced look it pairs well with 'cooler' evergreens such as lime-leafed *Pittosporum* or silver *Brachyglottis*.

Phormiums can be eye-catching, too. From a relatively small gene pool this New Zealand native has borne plants in reds, pinks, oranges, purples and greens. Some forms are stronger than others. *Phormium . cookianum* 'Tricolor' has a hummocked habit and perma-fresh lolloping leaves in stripes of red, green and cream. *P.* 'Evening Glow' is more upright and thrusting with mid-pink, watermelon-coloured leaves trimmed in pale brown – not one for the faint-hearted. Perhaps the brightest of all, with dangerously yellow leaves sporting the occasional green stripe, is *P.* 'Yellow Wave'. Despite its near overbearing colour, its relaxed habit and movement stops it being a jarring, yellow blob on the landscape.

Cordylines, or cabbage palms, as they are known, make handsome spot plants or fine container specimens thanks to their symmetrical silhouette. The straight species of *Cordyline australis*, with its mid-green leaves and palmy look, stands tall and fresh through winter, but I avoid the purple/burgundy-leafed forms because these have a certain muted flatness of colour and just don't feel very alive. *C.* 'Cherry Sensation' (below), however, is a dramatic red-pink cultivar which zings with colour year-round. Like several of the more exotically coloured cordylines, it's likely to suffer in very cold conditions so needs to be sited in a protected area close to the house.

The blades of all these spikey New Zealanders clatter around in the breeze, but for more soothing auditory tones bamboos and grasses hit the right note. Through autumn and winter the russet, orange and brown leaves of the pheasant grass, *Anemanthele lessoniana*, maintain an irrepressible form and emit soft rustling sounds. This grass is a perfect foil to late chrysanthemums, after which it carries its autumnal hues through till spring. It has a habit of occasionally seeding around, which is a blessing rather than a burden as it can pop up in surprisingly well-chosen spots.

A smaller 365-day grass is *Carex*, but choosing the best species of this plant can be a challenge. Some, such as *C.* 'Evergold', are depressingly unchanging and may as well be plastic for all the season variance they show. Others, such as *C. flagellifera* are washed-out brown-greys that can suck the life out of the garden faster than a patch of bare soil. Perhaps the most vibrant and life giving is *C. testacea*, with its mid-brown leaves burnished with orange and the pale-leaved *C. comans* 'Frosted Curls'. 'Frosted Curls' with its delicate cream variegation.

Of all the 'bladed' or monocotyledonous plants, bamboos are certainly the biggest and arguably the most dramatic. Some do feel like bog-standard, dark-leaved evergreens, but several bring colour to the garden year-round in both their foliage and sometimes in their canes, too. *Fargesia murielae* 'Bimbo' is a delicate-leaved, truly dwarf bamboo reaching no more than 1 metre in height and spread. It provides good groundcover and holds its colour year-round, but for real drama the wordily titled *Phyllostachys aureosulcata* f. *aureocaulis* is the ticket. This lofty bamboo can reach 6 metres and needs retaining with a purpose-made root barrier to reign in its desire for world domination! Its thick canes glow with yellow-orange tones through the year and if you're lucky it produces arty-looking longitudinal green stripes on its lower stems. Other, more dwarfing cultivars such as the cream and green variegated *Pleioblastus variegatus* don't run and only reach 40–80cm.

Top left Yucca 'Color Guard' holds its own through the seasons without a down day.

Top right Phormium 'Evening Glow'. Other cultivars range from purples, pinks and cream to red and near black.

Bottom left Phormium cookianum 'Tricolor' is reliably bright and less rigid than the P. tenax cultivars.

Bottom right Bright bamboos such as *Phyllostachys aureosulcata* f. *aureocaulis* work well in larger gardens.

Evergreen ferns such as *Polystichum setiferum* (Divisilobum Group) and *Asplenium scolopendrium* bring year-round colour to shady areas.

365-day ferns and palms

Long before bamboos arrived on the planet a mere 40 million years ago, ferns were growing, evolving and bringing colour, albeit mainly green, to the planet. Of the evergreen ferns, I most often plant *Polystichum setiferum* (Divisilobum Group) – soft shield fern is easier to remember. It's the most forgiving, gentle, subtly coloured fern I've grown, and it barely doffs its cap to winter, carrying on regardless of temperature or light. Its fronds are mid-green but appear even lighter thanks to their fine hairs and pleasing orange-brown stems. Grow it in part to full shade on most soils.

Asplenium scolopendrium has quite a different look, with its leathery un-dissected leaves. These form a glossy tussock of mid-green year-round, but this fern is much improved with a shear in spring. Doing this allows its newly formed fronds to emerge unfettered by last season's growth. It's a European native and fairly unfussy as to its location and soil. *Polypodium vulgare* is also a worthwhile year-rounder, with a squat form, light green, ladder-like foliage and the capacity to thrive in dry shade.

Most of these 365-day ferns are ideal for groundcover, but for larger architectural form and colour I turn to the palms. Some of their clan, such as the bone-hardy *Trachycarpus fortunei*, fall into the dark-evergreen bracket, but a few, such as *Chamaerops humilis* var. *cerifera* (right) are altogether cheerier. This dwarf palm is not a tough as *T. fortunei*, but through the year it holds its leaf stems skyward with minimal winter droop and has an appealing pale blue-grey hue. It's perfect to plunge into pots for summer; this way it can be moved to warmer spots closer to the house come winter.

TOP 40
365-DAY PLANTS

1. *Rosa* × *odorata* 'Bengal Crimson'
2. *Nandina domestica*
3. *Trachelospermum jasminoides*
4. *Phormium cookianum* 'Tricolor'
5. *Hebe* 'Heartbreaker'
6. *Epimedium* × *rubrum*
7. *Heuchera* 'Peach Flambé'
8. *Acca sellowiana*
9. *Bergenia purpurascens*
10. *Arbutus unedo* 'Compacta'
11. *Lophomyrtus* × *ralphii* 'Magic Dragon'
12. *Luma apiculata*
13. *Sedum telephium*
14. *Buxus sempervirens* 'Aureovariegata'
15. *Anemanthele lessoniana*
16. *Yucca* 'Color Guard'
17. *Polystichum setiferum* (Divisilobum Group)
18. *Cryptomeria japonica* 'Vilmoriniana'
19. *Chamaerops humilis* var. *cerifera*
20. *Arum italicum*
21. *Rhus typhina*
22. *Ageratina ligustrina*
23. *Hebe* 'Silver Dollar'
24. *Eucalyptus gunnii*
25. *Cynara scolymus*
26. *Rumex sanguineus* var. *sanguineus*
27. *Choisya ternata* Sundance
28. *Phormium tenax* cultivars
29. *Rubus cockburnianus*
30. *Mahonia eurybracteata* subsp. *ganpinensis* 'Soft Caress'
31. *Betula ermanii*
32. *Acer davidii*
33. *Persicaria affinis*
34. *Pittosporum tobira*
35. *Hebe ochracea* 'James Stirling'
36. *Hedera colchica* 'Sulphur Heart'
37. *Hedera helix* 'Little Diamond'
38. *Juniperus* sp.
39. *Pyracantha* sp.
40. *Lonicera nitida* 'Baggesen's Gold'

SUMMER PLANTS

EARLY SUMMER

Meconopsis cambrica
'Frances Perry'

Meconopsis have a reputation as being difficult and demanding, but not this one. Hailing from Wales, it out-flowers other meconopsis and most poppy relatives by some months and is easy to grow. Established in moisture-retentive soil with dappled light it will flower non-stop (unless the season is very dry) from early summer to autumn. It gently self-sows, picking and choosing its own perfect spots, and will stay true orange-red so long as there are no other forms nearby. Try dotting a few plants through a dappled shade area and let nature take its course.

H/S 50cm × 40cm
Season of colour: Fls: spring, summer, autumn; Fol: spring–autumn
Colour combination: light yellow-green/blue/violet/light yellow
Grow it with: *Euphorbia amygdaloides* var. *robbiae*
Follow-on plant: *Strobilanthes atropurpurea* (also flowers in unison)

Verbascum phoeniceum
'Violetta'

V. 'Violetta' is a delicate mullein that was discovered in the wild a few years back. It seems to be stable and comes true from its own seed, unless you let it cross with other verbascum, in which case you may strike gold with a stunning new hybrid. Shorter than other mulleins, this plant will reach around 70cm but can quickly wither if other species lollop onto its basal rosette of dark leaves. The flowers are a true dark violet and will be produced most prolifically in full sun on free-draining soil. Try it in gravel or towards the border front, backed by pale plants, to show off its rich tones.

H/S 70cm × 40cm
Season of colour: Fls: summer; Fol: spring–autumn
Colour combination: yellow-green/silver/pink/orange/pink-purple
Grow it with: *Dahlia* 'Peach Brandy'
Follow-on plant: *Verbena bonariensis*

Potentilla × hopwoodiana

This charming border-front perennial still has something of the wild about it, with its rambling stems and speckling, rather than splattering, of flowers. Appearing from early summer until mid-autumn, blooms are intricately complex with an outer ring of light red-pink giving way to an inner pale-pink blush, which is centred with red. It favours a sunny site and free-draining soil. Flowering slows at certain points in summer and it won't always re-flower from a cut back, so it is best left alone. Though it can add bounty to border fronts it's also good elevated in rock gardens or banks where its special flowers can be viewed eye to eye.

H/S 20cm × 1m
Season of colour: Fls: summer; Fol: spring–autumn
Colour combination: yellow-green/silver/pink/orange/pink-purple
Grow it with: *Artemisia ludoviciana* 'Valerie Finnis'
Follow-on plant: *Eucomis bicolor*

Linaria 'Peachy'

I've only known this toadflax cultivar for two years but it has proved its worth so far, flowering with abandon, like the wild species, summer-long. Its flowers are held on top of grey-green willow-leaved stems in racemes with individual blooms resembling mini tight-lipped snapdragons. The colour is something special, too. Flowers are essentially a light yellow with dabs of red-pink which optically blend to create … you've guessed it – peach. Establishing them takes significant watering in the first season but following that they get by on their own, doing best in full sun on a free-draining soil. Their elegant, swaying columnar habit means they are perfect in herbaceous borders, slotted twixt larger-leafed plants.

H/S 1m × 40cm
Season of colour: Fls: spring–summer; Fol: spring–autumn
Colour combination: light yellow/pink/violet/pink-purple
Grow it with: *Knautia macedonica*
Follow-on plant: *Gladiolus murielae*

Cirsium rivulare 'Atropurpureum'

Bees flock to the dark purple-red flowers of this stocky thistle. Forming a rounded basal clump of foliage, it sends up its first batch of 1-metre tall flowering stems in early summer followed by a second flush later on, so long as it's cut back. It's one of those see-through plants which works well mid-border where other plants can be viewed through its lofty stems. A free-draining but moisture-retentive soil in full sun will keep it happy. Split the plant every four years or so to maintain vigour and flowering. *Cirsium tuberosum*, a UK native, is similar in form, if a little less floriferous, and carries pink-violet flowers.

H/S 1.5m × 80cm
Season of colour: Fls: summer–early autumn; Fol: spring–autumn
Colour combination: light blue/light pink/violet/orange
Grow it with: *Linaria purpurea*
Follow-on plant: *Aster × frikartii* 'Mönch'

Penstemon
'Garnet'

It's hard to go wrong with penstemons. True, the occasional poor-performing cultivar makes it to the nurseries, but for reliable long-season colour they're a must. P. 'Garnet' is a narrow-leaved, stocky plant that musters a summer of darkest pink-red flowers with only the occasional week off. P. 'Alice Hindley' is a taller, more willowy plant with light blue-violet flowers. P. 'Hidcote Pink' is a mid-red-pink and highly floriferous. All are worth a grow and propagate easily from cuttings. They hold their foliage over winter, providing roots and lower stems with protection, so do not cut them back till mid-spring. Grow them on most soils in full sun.

H/S 70cm × 50cm
Season of colour: Fls: summer–early autumn; Fol: year-round
Colour combination: light blue/light pink/violet/orange
Grow it with: *Gaura lindheimeri* 'Siskiyou Pink'
Follow-on plant: *Aster* × *frikartii* 'Mönch'

Argyranthemum frutescens subsp. canariae

Parent to numerous cultivars, this classic marguerite comes from the Canary Islands where it enjoys a virtually frost-free existence. Starting in early summer it will flower till late autumn or beyond if brought into a cool glasshouse. Its white daisy flowers are standard fare, but are much improved by the plants feathery grey-green foliage. Prune it back hard in spring, reducing stems to half their length so the plant stays well foliated and dense with flowers. Grow it as a specimen plant in a large terracotta pot or plunge plastic-potted plants into beds for the season. Inevitably it needs full sun and a free-draining soil.

H/S 1m × 1m
Season of colour: Fls: summer–early autumn; Fol: year-round (protected)
Colour combination: light yellow/orange/blue/pink/purple
Grow it with: *Agapanthus* sp.
Follow-on plant: *Chrysanthemum* sp. to replace the daisy prior to the frosts

Clematis 'Perle d'Azur'

With flowering extending from midsummer to autumn (with a couple of weeks off in late summer) this enthusiastic clematis has earned its place as a garden classic. Flowers have an irresistible light violet-blue hue, centred with pale lime-white, and sit comfortably next to virtually any colour you care to try. It's a group 3 clematis, meaning pruning is simply cutting all its stems back to around 30cm in late winter. It likes its 3-metre and taller stems in the sun and its roots in the shade, or at least kept cool, so it benefits from a regular mulch at the base.

H/S 3m × 3m
Season of colour: Fls: summer–early autumn; Fol: spring–early autumn
Colour combination: pink/violet/light yellow/light green/dark purple-red
Grow it with: *Rosa* Tess of the d'Urbervilles
Follow-on plant: *Clematis tangutica*

Rosa
Graham Thomas

Named after one of England's
great plantsmen, this long-
flowering rose is a garden
stalwart. It has a bushy habit,
good scent and an old-fashioned
look thanks to the horticultural
alchemists at David Austin Roses.
Flowers emerge a strong yellow,
fading gracefully to a paler shade.
It is quick to establish and for this
reason benefits from deep
planting and basal staking to
avoid the large canopy being
bashed around in the wind
before the roots have taken hold.
Pruning is simply a matter of a
one third reduction of the crown
in late winter. Another long-
flowering rose of real merit is *R.*
'The Fairy'. It's a ground-hugging
plant with fine leaves and delicate
pink, button-sized blooms.

H/S 1.3m × 1.3m
Season of colour: Fls: early
summer–autumn; Fol: spring–
autumn
Colour combination: violet/
orange-brown/yellow-green/
grey-blue/blue
Grow it with: *Anchusa azurea*
'Londdon Royalist' and/or *Achillea*
'Terracotta'
Follow-on plant: *Galanthus* sp.

Salvia nemorosa
'Ostfriesland'

Few other plants have the neatness of form and longevity of colour
bestowed on this useful salvia. Rather than the dark amorphous-blob
effect that some floriferous blue plants suffer, this cultivar has pink
bracts which set off and define the blue. Some suggest a cut-back
after the first flush of flowers but I've found it to perform well left to
its own devices. It tolerates most free-draining soils and will flower
prolifically in full blazing sunshine. It works well planted in ribbon
swathes through herbaceous plantings where it provides a consistent
supply of colour through the growing season.

H/S 45cm × 40cm
Season of colour: Fls: early summer–autumn; Fol: spring–autumn
Colour combination: violet/purple/light yellow/light orange/pink
Grow it with: *Anthemis tinctoria* 'E.C. Buxton'
Follow-on plant: *Colchicum autumnale*

10
MORE EARLY SUMMER PLANTS

1. *Lavandula stoechas*
2. *Erigeron annuus*
3. *Galega officinalis*
4. *Osteospermum jucundum*
5. *Lespedeza thunbergii*
6. *Centaurea montana*
7. *Convolvulus cneorum*
8. *Anthemis tinctoria* 'E.C. Buxton'
9. *Cistus × pulverulentus* 'Sunset'
10. *Lysimachia ephemerum*

MID-SUMMER

Cosmos atrosanguineus

Blessed with a dark-chocolate aroma this Mexican tenderish perennial glistens in the harsh midday sunlight and disappears into the background by dusk. I've noticed distinct forms of the plant over the years – some lanky and liable to lollop, others better with shorter internodes and flowers displayed in a dome. *C. atrosanguineus* Chocamocha is quite a good selection but the straight species can be as good if you find an upstanding floriferous form. Once you've got a good one, be sure to propagate from it. Simple cuttings taken in late summer and kept light and frost-free over winter will do the trick. Nestled between 40–50cm perennials or lightly supported with pea sticks it will flower like its very close cousin, the dahlia, from midsummer till the frosts.

H/S 60cm × 40cm
Season of colour: Fls: summer–autumn; Fol: summer–autumn
Colour combination: violet/purple/red/pink-purple
Grow it with: *Potentilla atrosanguinea* or *Sedum* 'Matrona'
Follow-on plant: *Erysimum cheiri* 'Vulcan' (covers – autumn/winter)

Phygelius aequalis
'New Sensation'

Known as the Cape fuchsia, this beautiful tubular-flowered plant is but one of thousands of unique species to originate from the Cape province of South Africa. It has woody bases to its stems, so when grown in the northern hemisphere it is often referred to as a woody perennial. Like penstemons, it should not be cut back in autumn but rather left with its near-evergreen structure unpruned till spring. Flower colour is as described – sensational with a pink-purple hue. Starting in midsummer it will flower till the frosts. Grow in moisture-retentive but free-draining soil in full sun.

H/S 60cm × 40cm
Season of colour: Fls: summer–autumn; Fol: year-round
Colour combination: yellow-green/dark pink-violet/violet
Grow it with: *Geranium pratense* 'Plenum Violaceum'
Follow-on plant: *Callicarpa bodinieri* var. *giraldii* 'Profusion'

Diascia personata

Flowering for five months or more, this sun-loving plant falls somewhere between perennial and tender perennial. Cuttings taken in summer serve as insurance, but when grown in a free-draining soil in full sun with plenty of air movement it will survive a few sub-zero nights. The flowers are a cheery red-pink and neatly stacked up the stem. Though it looks well in a border setting, the surrounding plants can cause the diascia to lollop. This is not such a problem and can lead to some inspiring combinations as unexpected stems cross. However, pea-sticking early in the season makes for a smarter upright plant.

H/S 1m x 50cm
Season of colour: Fls: summer–autumn; Fol: spring–autumn
Colour combination: violet/purple/blue/yellow-green
Grow it with: *Campanula lactiflora*
Follow-on plant: *Miscanthus* 'Purpurascens'

Knautia macedonica

For an unadulterated wild thing this long-flowering perennial is very well behaved. It produces a succession of purple-red button flowers balanced on slender stems above the foliage. Blooming in flushes from early summer to mid-autumn it comes close to competing with its long-flowering cousin *Scabiosa caucasica* 'Clive Greaves'. Unlike some of the scabious, it requires little staking, unless the season is very wet, in which case a few cunningly placed pea sticks will keep the mound of stems from collapsing. Grow it in full sun on a moisture-retentive but free-draining soil. Watering and mulching around the base will reduce the chances of powdery mildew. Deadhead to prolong its flowering season.

H/S 80cm x 80cm
Season of colour: Fls: summer–autumn; Fol: spring–autumn
Colour combination: light blue/light violet/light pink/grey-blue/blue
Grow it with: *Stipa tenuissima*
Follow-on plant: *Stipa tenuissima*

Phlox drummondii 'Moody Blues'

This small annual phlox should really be called 'Moody Violets' as it's not truly blue but very slightly infused with red, creating a delicious optical mix of hues as every plant in a batch of seed is slightly different. For this reason, they work best planted en masse to achieve an overall colour effect. Despite the fact that they begin life as unpromising leggy seedling, they rapidly bulk up and flower their hearts out from early summer to the frosts. They look great fronting perennial borders but work just as well around the edge of containers where they complement virtually every colour. Grow them in full sun on a moisture-retentive but free-draining soil.

H/S 25cm x 30cm
Season of colour: Fls: summer–autumn; Fol: late spring–autumn
Colour combination: dark pink/green/light yellow/purple/violet
Grow it with: *Argyranthemum* Madeira Crested Merlot
Follow-on plant: *Erysimum cheiri* (orange)

Cleome hassleriana
'Violet Queen'

The dark pink-violet flowers of this South American annual are irresistibly exotic with their over-sized stamens and elegant almond-shaped petals. Such is its vigour that this mere annual can easily hold its own, in groups of five or more, in perennial borders or amongst the bold foliage of exotic plantings. The flowering stems continue to extend from midsummer till late autumn with a succession of blooms providing real flower power. It's a hungry plant, so grow it in full sun in a soil enriched with compost or manure. Keep the watering up to avoid powdery mildew and stake plants in midsummer to stop them becoming top heavy.

H/S 1.2m × 40cm
Season of colour: Fls: summer–autumn; Fol: spring–autumn
Colour combination: red/light yellow/pale blue/yellow-green/white
Grow it with: *Nicotiana langsdorffii*
Follow-on plant: *Helianthus* 'Lemon Queen'

Nicotiana 'Lime Green'

Very few ornamental plants produce glowing green flowers, so those which do ought to be cherished. *N.* 'Lime Green' is one such plant. It carries flowers of a zingy, yet accommodating, green which are able to flatter and enliven most other colours. Like all other nicotianas, this one germinates and bulks up fast so it doesn't need sowing till mid-spring. Grown on a windowsill or under glass it's ready for planting by late spring once the frosts have passed. It needs full sun to thrive and regular feeding to ensure a succession of blooms till early autumn. Place it with other vibrant annuals in a herbaceous border or as a 'one-size-fits-all' filler plant.

H/S 40cm × 40cm
Season of colour: Fls: summer–autumn; Fol: late spring–autumn
Colour combination: red/yellow/pink/orange/purple/blue/violet/white
Grow it with: *Calendula officinalis*
Follow-on plant: *Tulipa humilis* 'Persian Pearl' (planted when the nicotiana is lifted in autumn)

Lopezia cordata 'Pretty Rose'

Relatively unknown, this quirky little Mexican annual blooms for five months or more. Direct-sown in mid-spring into shallow furrows on a prepared piece of soil, it needs little more than watering in the weeks before and after germination. Following this it quickly bulks up to a neat bun shape, flowering some 70 days later. It's commonly known as mosquito flower – there must be a more glamorous comparator? Flower colour is a mix of pale and dark pinks with a smattering of everything in between. Grow it as an 'edger', where it will do a good 'front-of-house' job ahead of taller annuals and perennials.

H/S 30cm × 30cm
Season of colour: Fls: summer–autumn; Fol: summer–autumn
Colour combination: silver/purple/dark pink/grey-blue/violet
Grow it with: *Cerinthe major* 'Purpurascens'
Follow-on plant: *Colchicum autumnale* 'Water Lily'

Hemerocallis 'Stella de Oro'

Day lilies come from China and Japan, but today it's the Americans who worship this plucky perennial, breeding hundreds of cultivars from lilac to red. *H.* 'Stella de Oro' is one such plant. Its petals don't have the spidery elegance of some forms but it's arguably the longest-flowering. Foliage appears in early spring, quickly forming a neat mound from which arise short stems loaded with a succession of day-long blooms. It is a very tolerant plant; I've grown it in most soils in dappled shade to full sun and even in grassy meadows, where it naturally occurs. Grown at the border front it will perform from summer till late autumn.

H/S 50cm × 50cm
Season of colour: Fls: summer–autumn; Fol: early spring–winter
Colour combination: red/silver/blue/violet/orange/yellow
Grow it with: *Delphinium* 'Bruce'
Follow-on plant: *Liriope muscari* (some cross over in flowering)

Isotoma axillaris 'Indigo Stars'

I've sown and grown this perfect little annual for the last 15 years and its floriferous nature continues to impress me. Various versions of it have appeared over that time, with *I.* 'Indigo Stars' the latest refinement. From an early sowing, under glass or on a windowsill, it takes around 100 days to flower. Once planted out in pots or as a border 'fronter' it will form a symmetrical tortoise-sized tussock of foliage and bloom. Flowers are evenly spaced and blue-violet in colour. It does have a dark secret, though, it's poisonous, so a hand wash after contact is essential.

H/S 25cm × 30cm
Season of colour: Fls: summer–autumn; Fol: summer–autumn
Colour combination: red/silver/violet/light brown-orange/purple
Grow it with: *Verbena* 'Peaches 'n' Cream'
Follow-on plant: *Viola wittrockiana* (for bedding areas and pots)

10
MORE MID-SUMMER PLANTS

1. *Brugmansia sanguinea*
2. *Salvia sclarea* var. *turkestanica*
3. *Verbena hastata*
4. *Eryngium × tripartitum*
5. *Francoa sonchifolia*
6. *Sanguisorba officinalis* (June–October)
7. *Aster × frikartii* 'Mönch'
8. *Veronicastrum virginicum* 'Fascination'
9. *Monarda* 'Violet Queen'
10. *Eccremocarpus scaber*

LATE SUMMER

Canna × ehemanii

Canna's bold flowers and foliage bring a rush of exuberance to the frazzled late-summer garden. I used to treat these spreading vertical perennials like dahlias, dutifully lifting and storing them in autumn. However, forms such as *C. × ehemanii* are that bit hardier and can see out winter in-situ under a rain-protecting mulch capping, so long as they are in full sun on a free-draining soil. Unlike many of the highly bred forms, this plant has a certain grace, with lax, well-spaced, dark red-pink flowers. Another irresistible cultivar is *C.* 'Panache' with open, multi-tonal, red-pink flowers and pointy leaves with a glaucous hint. Split for propagation in early spring.

H/S 2.2m × 1m
Season of colour: Fls: summer–autumn; Fol: summer–autumn
Colour combination: purple/silver/light pink/yellow
Grow it with: *Impatiens tinctoria*
Follow-on plant: *Leptospermum* 'Silver Sheen'

Cobaea scandens

This climber may be known as the cup and saucer vine but cream teas and cucumber sandwiches it isn't! Bestowed with chunky violet flowers and cream stamens in a spidery tangle this plant is truly tropical. Sown in February, under glass, it takes five months to flower, but it's worth the wait. Unusually, the flowers have four beautiful stages. Unopened they form a pale green balloon, followed by the violet cup flower, then the saucer sepal and finally lozenge-shaped seed pods. Sold as an annual, it's actually a perennial, which I've got to survive through numerous winters on a south-facing wall. Full sun and rich, free-draining soil is essential.

H/S 7m × 2–3m
Season of colour: Fls: summer–autumn; Fol: summer–autumn
Colour combination: orange/pink/silver/light yellow/red
Grow it with: *Eccremocarpus scaber*
Follow-on plant: *Narcissus* 'Spellbinder'

Crocosmia
'Lucifer'

Well-known to gardeners who crave late-summer opulence, this reliable corm is distinctly architectural in foliage and flower. Well before its stems, like long-necked birds, reveal their true red flowers, its foliage holds its own in the border. Ribbed mid-green leaves have a broad-sword look and work well clumped among earlier flowerers, ready to replace the colour gap as they fade in late summer. Combine it with purple-red foliage plants, blues and oranges, but I avoid strong yellow, which can cheapen its look. Best grown in full sun on a moisture-retentive but free-draining soil. Light staking support early in the year will prevent the clump collapsing.

H/S 1.2m × 1m
Season of colour: Fls: summer; Fol: spring–autumn
Colour combination: purple-red/blue/orange/blue-violet
Grow it with: *Eryngium bourgatii* 'Picos Amethyst'
Follow-on plant: *Chrysanthemum* 'Mary Stoker'

Euphorbia schillingii

By late summer some euphorbias look a bit frazzled, but *E. schillingii* toughs it out, staying fresh into autumn. Stems are ringed with layers of mid-green foliage highlighted with a white strip on each of the leaves' midribs. This, coupled with fresh yellow-green bracted flowers, makes this reliable perennial feel like a spring thing. Grow it in light dappled shade on a relatively free-draining soil. Like the early-flowering euphorbias before it, this plant adds a zingy edge to other surrounding plants, especially those with orange or blue flowers. The white midrib on the leaves can be picked out by planting white-flowered *Aster divaricatus* nearby.

H/S 1m × 80cm
Season of colour: Fls: summer–autumn; Fol: spring–autumn
Colour combination: blue/orange/blue-violet/red/white
Grow it with: *Aster divaricatus*
Follow-on plant: *Hyacinthoides non-scripta*

Dahlia
'Honka'

D. 'Honka' almost doesn't look like a dahlia, with its reflexed petals and light yellow starry faces. Grow it, and other cultivars, on an enriched, moisture-retentive soil in full sun. Staking is essential for taller forms and they all bloom better with regular deadheading. Plant tubers in late spring, protecting against molluscs, and lift, dry and store over winter where soil sits wet and cold. Vilnius University Botanic Garden, in Lithuania, dedicates acres to hundreds of dahlia cultivars. This landscape of colour is dramatic, but in private gardens dahlias are best paired with other, more subtle, plants to avoid a fight for attention. *D.* 'David Howard' (burnt orange), *D.* 'Bishop of Dover' (white with a hint of violet) and *D.* 'Chat Noir' (dark purple-brown) are other favourites.

H/S 1m × 80cm
Season of colour: Fls: summer–autumn; Fol: summer–autumn
Colour combination: blue/orange/blue-violet/white/green
Grow it with: *Gaura lindheimeri*
Follow-on plant: *Allium* 'Globemaster'

Lobelia x speciosa 'Russian Princess'

Until late summer the leafy deep-purple columnar spires of this lobelia fade in the shadows unless they're paired with silver. Then suddenly, ka-pow!, spires of electrified pink-purple flowers, unrivalled by any other, appear. It needs a site in sun to dappled shade with moist soil in summer and a relatively free-draining one in winter – a challenge best rectified by adding grit at planting to ensure winter drainage and then watering well in summer. Slugs and snails can also be a problem during establishment, so take measures to prevent them. Ok, it can be a pain to maintain, but for that unrivalled colour, it's worth it.

H/S 1m × 45cm
Season of colour: Fls: late summer–autumn; Fol: spring–autumn
Colour combination: blue-violet/green/light pink/purple/grey-blue
Grow it with: *Hosta sieboldiana* var. *elegans*
Follow-on plant: *Cardamine pratensis*

Amicia zygomeris

This tenderish Andean perennial is a horticultural curiosity, normally planted for background texture rather than colour. Flowers are pea-like, strong yellow and few and far between, so it's the plant's purple-veined stipules that I rely on to befriend anything in the purple floral spectrum that is situated nearby. Try it mixed up with purple-leaved *Atriplex hortensis* var. *rubra*, which has a similar form. Together the pair work to highlight pink tones in front of them. Grow it in full sun or it will become lanky and unable to support itself. It's happy on most soils but will overwinter best on a free-draining one.

H/S 2m × 1m
Season of colour: Fls: late summer–autumn; Fol: late spring–autumn
Colour combination: blue-violet/green/light pink/purple/grey-blue
Grow it with: *Dahlia* 'Fascination'
Follow-on plant: *Smyrnium perfoliatum*

Salvia patens

The bluest blue of all blues has to be this salvia. It virtually crackles with intensity – so much so that I've noted crowds gathering around it in public gardens – no, really. Its hooded blooms are large, for a salvia, with an almost felty quality. It's often grown as an annual but can be lifted and over-wintered frost-free. Cuttings in late summer are also a cinch. It's hard to think of a colour with which it does not sit with ease, except perhaps darkest violets and blues, which could swallow it up. Grow it in a free-draining but moisture-retentive soil in full sun. Wow.

H/S 70cm × 50cm
Season of colour: Fls: summer–autumn; Fol: spring–autumn
Colour combination: orange/green/light pink/red/white/yellow
Grow it with: *Tithonia rotundifolia*
Follow-on plant: *Tulipa* cultivars (planted as the salvia is lifted for winter)

Mirabilis jalapa

Like dahlias, these tuberous South American perennials take their time to come into bloom, but when they do their range of colour is sensational, from pinks and reds to orange and yellow. But, here lies a problem. Apart from a wishy-washy cultivar known as *M. j.* 'Buttermilk', I've found it all but impossible to source single colours of this intoxicatingly scented plant. To get around this I've grown, selected and sacrificed many. Treat them like dahlias in cold climes or grow in a warm spot with enriched soil and a mulch capping over winter. Perfect featured in late exotic plantings, their perfume appears from early evening.

H/S 1m × 70cm
Season of colour: Fls: late summer–autumn; Fol: late summer–autumn
Colour combination: dark green/purple/violet
Grow it with: *Ricinus communis*
Follow-on plant: *Nigella sativa* (flowers before the mirabilis appears)

10
MORE LATE SUMMER PLANTS

❶ *Helianthus salicifolius*

❷ *Abutilon* 'Canary Bird'

❸ *Phlox paniculata*

❹ *Aster divaricatus*

❺ *Begonia grandis subsp. evansiana*

❻ *Ammi visnaga*

❼ *Eupatorium purpureum* 'Atropurpureum'

❽ *Atriplex hortensis var. rubra*

❾ *Silybum marianum*

❿ *Monarda* 'Violet Queen'

Geranium × riversleaianum 'Russell Prichard'

Choose the right geraniums and you'll have a summer of colour without too much effort. *G.* Rozanne is rightfully the horticultural world's current darling, with up to eight months of mid-blue and white flowers struck through with ruddy venation. Similarly, *G.* 'Dilys' flowers for as many months in pale purple-pink, but is not as large or floriferous. However, I've most often relied on the classic *G.* 'Russell Prichard', which produces a burgeoning mass of soft grey-green foliage festooned with purple-pink flowers for up to five months. Like many geraniums, it's adaptable but is best grown on a well-drained but moisture-retentive soil in full sun. It's a classy border-fronter, or is equally at home spilling over a low wall.

H/S 30cm × 1m+
Season of colour: Fls: summer–autumn; Fol: spring–autumn
Colour combination: violet/purple/yellow-green/light blue
Grow it with: *Penstemon* 'Sour Grapes'
Follow-on plant: *Scilla siberica*

LONGEST FLOWERING PLANTS

THE LONGEST-FLOWERING PLANTS

One of the joys of gardening is savouring those ephemeral plants that only share their blooms for a matter of days. Little gems that have barely broken the soil surface before they return to hibernation demand attention and wonderment, but to have a 365-day garden it's not possible to rely on these plants alone. Colour stalwarts that can't help but bloom themselves into a frenzy are vital to keep the colour coming. I've tried and tested hundreds, maybe thousands, of plants over the years for their blooming power and garden worth. Some are launched amid a tide of enthusiasm from breeders only to perform poorly in the garden, others, like some of those listed in this chapter, go on to be classics. Weather, location and soil all play a role in a plant's capacity to perform, but with their basic needs met, the following species really deliver the goods for up to 12 months a year!

Achieving year-round colour is simplified by choosing certain key species that will flower for more than six months.

Rosa × odorata 'Bengal Crimson' (year-round)

This unsurpassed rose has the potential to flower every day of the year in a warm sheltered spot. Its single, true-red flowers flush heavily in late spring followed by a succession of blooms until late autumn, when the hue tones down to a dark pink throughout the winter months. No pruning required.

H/S 3.5m × 3.5m (though it will climb to 6m given the chance)
Grow it: in sun on a rich soil.

Euphorbia ceratocarpa (mid-spring–early winter)

With enough different species of euphorbia it's possible to have blooms nearly year-round, but *E. ceratocarpa* can cover spring to early winter on its own. It forms a block of foliage topped with a succession of yellow-green bracts and blooms. Leaves have a white midrib and a slim willowy grace about them.

H/S 1.3m × 1.3m
Grow it: in full sun on a free-draining soil

Erysimum 'Bowles's Mauve' (potentially year-round)

Ubiquity doesn't make this plant any less desirable. Along with its cousin, E. 'Apricot Twist', it is capable of year-round flowering in a sheltered spot and is much appreciated by pollinators. Flowers are in tones of light violet, altering with the seasons. It can flower itself to death, so taking cuttings is essential.

H/S 50cm × 50cm
Grow it: in full sun on a free-draining soil

Nemesia denticulata 'Confetti' (potentially year-round)

This extraordinary perennial is a tireless bloomer. It's flowered non-stop since I planted it in a sheltered London garden three years ago and shows no sign of burn-out. Occasional tidy-ups to remove tired stems and a feed once in a while see it outperform just about everything.

H/S 45cm × 45cm
Grow it: in full sun on most soils, bar those that sit wet in winter

Pelargonium (zonal) (mid-spring–late autumn, but potentially year-round)

This virtually un-killable popular balcony stalwart is highly bred but shows no weakness. Red-flowered forms are often the strongest and longest-lived. It's easy to propagate and can take a hack if it's getting out of hand. Drought or a two-week watering break cause it little bother.

H/S 45cm × 45cm
Grow it: in full sun on most soils, bar those that sit wet in winter

Geranium 'Dilys'
(late spring–late autumn)

Ok, so G. 'Dilys' can't compete with G. Rozanne for volume of flowers, but its gentle succession of small violet-pink blooms has an endearing cuteness, and its diminutive 'fingered' leaves make for a perfect foil. It's best grown as a border edger where beefier perennials can't overwhelm it.

H/S 30cm × 40cm

Grow it: in full sun on most soils, bar those that sit wet in winter

Rosa Pink Flower Carpet
(late spring–late autumn)

This compact groundcover rose is bred for long flowering and weed suppression, which it does with aplomb. It may not have the grace of older roses but eight months of flower and excellent disease resistance makes up for that. The pink form is strongest, in my experience, but white, amber and ruby shades are also available.

H/S 70cm × 1m

Grow it: in full sun on most soils with a manure mulch in spring

Daphne × transatlantica Eternal Fragrance
(late spring–early autumn)

Though its most dramatic flush of flowers appear in spring, this useful daphne continues to pop buds through till autumn. Blooms are palest pink with a reasonable scent. It's compact enough to grow in a container but will also work mid-border or as a low dividing hedge.

H/S 1m × 1m

Grow it: in woodsy soil in full sun or part-shade

Geranium Rozanne (late spring–late autumn)

Voted plant of the century by the RHS, it's difficult to find fault with this enthusiastic geranium. Its pale blue flowers are centred with white which is streaked through with red-brown navigation lines to direct would-be pollinators to the good stuff. Its habit is like a squat cumulus cloud and it will tumble over a wall to great effect.

H/S 50cm × 1m

Grow it: in full sun on most moisture-retentive but free-draining soils

Corydalis lutea
(mid-spring–late autumn)
At home in cracks and crevices, gravel and at the base of walls, this corydalis is a welcome migrant that often arrives of its own volition. Strong yellow flowers decorate its tight dome of dissected foliage for months on end. Allow it to self-seed and edit at will.
H/S 20cm × 20cm
Grow it: in full sun or part-shade in free-draining soil

Erigeron karvinskianus
(late spring–late autumn)
Once this delicate daisy has a foothold in the garden it will pick its favoured spots and proliferate. It self-seeds freely into gravel, paving and walls where its white flowers, which fade to myriad shades of pink, can add a hint of wildness to more formal areas.
H/S 20cm × 20cm
Grow it: in full sun in free-draining soil

Erigeron glaucus
(early summer–late autumn)
There is much to admire in this coastal fat-headed daisy. It's compact, yet manages to draw in pollinators and people alike as it cloakes the soil at the border front. Foliage is evergreen (pale green-blue) giving it 365-day appeal. Wild and some cultivated forms self-seed into desirable cracks and crevices.
H/S 20cm × 50cm
Grow it: in full sun in a free-draining soil

Salvia nemorosa 'Ostfriesland' **(late spring–early autumn)**
Not many gardens I've designed escape without this plant appearing somewhere. Its violet-blue flowers and purple bracts persist for five months or more on compact, upright plants. Grow it for drama en masse in the middle of borders. Essential.
H/S 45cm × 40cm
Grow it: in full sun in free-draining but moisture-retentive soil

Pelargonium 'Surcouf' (ivy-leafed trailing)
(early summer–late autumn)
Lots of the ivy-leafed pelargoniums will flower for six months or more, but the colour of this cultivar is just irresistible. With a dark pink to magenta base the petals also carry tones of violet and red. It looks amazing grown as a pot specimen and complements virtually any colour you care to put its way.
H/S 35cm × 1m+
Grow it: in full sun in free-draining but moisture-retentive soil and feed regularly

Osteospermum jucundum (late spring–mid-autumn)
Forming a near weed-proof mat of foliage, this South African daisy has moments of explosive flowering, but its residual setting is a slow succession of blooms through most of its season. Flowers fade through shades of pale pink with the slightest hint of violet. It's a perfect border-fronter in dry plantings.
H/S 20cm × 1m+
Grow it: in full sun in free-draining soil

Fuchsia magellanica
(late spring–early winter)
Hailing from South America, this wild fuchsia positively drips with flowers through summer and autumn. Cultivars such as the white F. 'Hawkshead' are equally floriferous and provide flower power that is a little less run-of-the-mill. Hard-prunes every other year keeps this woody shrub fresh and free-flowering.
H/S 2m × 1.5m
Grow it: in full sun to dappled in most soils

Viburnum tinus (winter–late-spring)
Often cited as the UK's longest-flowering shrub, this white-bloomed evergreen viburnum and its cultivars, such as V. 'Eve Price', are useful stalwarts. Unopened buds dot the shrub with pink 'berries' for some time before they open. Fruits appear after the flowers in a deep metallic blue.
H/S 3m × 2m
Grow it: in full sun in most soils

Geum 'Totally Tangerine'
(late spring–autumn)
Surpassing other geums and potentillas, this vigorous, healthy hybrid cultivar is an essential border or container plant. It's a tireless flower factory, churning out multi-tonal brown-orange blooms for up to seven months with minimal care and attention. Pair it with purples and magentas for drama or silvers to balance its 'heat'.
H/S 50cm × 50cm
Grow it: in full sun in moisture-retentive but free-draining soil

Weigela 'All Summer Red'
(late spring–mid-autumn)
New on the scene, this plant is a developed cultivar of the old garden favourite. It's oddly compact for a weigela and has not been around long enough to prove its long-term merits, but it appears to do what its sellers claim and flowers for around 5–6 months.
H/S 2m x 1.5m
Grow it: in full sun in most soils

Salvia × jamensis cultivars
(late spring–late autumn)
The numerous cultivars of this reliable hybrid range between pale and dark pinks to violet and yellow. The red and white S. 'Hot Lips' is de rigueur but I prefer the primrose-yellow S. 'La Luna'. Left unpruned and with winter protection these shrubby salvias can flower for 7–8 months.
H/S 1.2m x 1.2m
Grow it: in full sun in well-fed but free-draining soil

Viola tricolor
(late spring–early winter)
The parent of numerous cultivars, this cheery-faced viola can flower relentlessly for 7–8 months. Its colour mix of violet, white and yellow has a clean feel and works as a foil to potted evergreens. It will seed around nicely in wilder areas. For best value, grow it from seed.
H/S 30cm x 30cm
Grow it: in sun or part-shade on all but the driest soils

Erodium chrysanthum
(early summer– late autumn)
With its silver dissected foliage and palest yellow flowers, this erodium is hard not to like, especially when you know it can flower its way through summer and autumn. E. 'Country Park' is a pink selection with similar longevity. Grow it in gravel, in paving cracks or at the front of a xerophytic (drought resistant) planting.
H/S 20cm x 40cm
Grow it: in full sun in a fast-draining soil

Verbena bonariensis
(early summer– late autumn)

Over-wintered plants of this popular tender perennial will flower in late spring while stronger self-seeded plants will begin blooming in early summer. After 20 years in the limelight it's no longer uber-fashionable but is a boon for longevity and loved by pollinators. It's the classic 'see-through' plant that's at home anywhere in a border.

H/S 1.5m × 60cm

Grow it: in full sun on moisture-retentive but free-draining soil

UP TO 6 MONTHS' FLOWERING

- *Fragaria* 'Lipstick' (late spring–early autumn)
- *Coreopsis sp.* (early summer–mid-autumn)
- *Diascia personata* (early summer–mid-autumn)
- *Heuchera* 'Ginger Snap' (mid-spring–mid-autumn)
- *Fremontodendron californicum* (late spring–early autumn)
- *Clematis* Fleuri (or any of the boulevard forms) (mid-spring–late summer)
- *Grevillea rosmarinifolia* (late winter–early summer)
- *Dianthus* EverLast™ Burgundy Blush (early summer–mid-autumn)
- *Hydrangea* 'Wim's Red' (early summer–late autumn)
- *Potentilla fruticosa* 'Abbotswood' (late spring–early autumn)
- *Knautia macedonica* (late spring–mid-autumn)
- *Aster* × *frikartii* 'Mönch' (midsummer–late autumn)
- *Eryngium* × *tripartitum* (early summer–mid-autumn)
- *Gaura lindheimeri* (early summer–late autumn)
- *Centranthus ruber* (late spring–early autumn)
- *Astrantia sp.* (late spring–early autumn with rests)
- *Scabiosa* 'Butterfly Blue' (early summer–late autumn)
- *Antirrhinum braun-blanquetii* (late spring–early autumn)
- *Nemesia* Maritana Sky Lagoon (early summer–mid-autumn)
- *Diascia* Little Dreamer (early summer–mid-autumn)
- **Bedding annuals:** *Impatiens, Tagetes, Lobelia, Petunia, Verbena, Bidens, Surfinia* (early summer– mid-autumn)
- *Verbena hastata* (midsummer–late autumn)
- *Meconopsis cambrica* (mid-spring–early autumn)
- *Astrantia* 'Roma' (late spring–autumn)
- *Kniphofia* 'Creamsicle' (summer–late autumn)
- *Corydalis ochroleuca* (spring–autumn)

EXTEND THE
SEASON

EXTEND EITHER END *of the* SEASON...

...with the earliest- and latest-flowering versions of garden favourites

Choose the right roses and it's possible to have these garden stalwarts in flower for up to 9 months of the year, right up until early winter.

Daffodils just flower in spring, right? Well, lots of them do, but that's not the whole story. Like roses, clematis and other garden staples, daffodils have a well-known peak season, but some special members of their clan flower long before or long after the bulk of them. This means that by adding a few special plants to the garden it's possible to have daffodils flowering across seven months of the year, from late autumn to early summer. It might seem far-fetched, but it's pretty easy to do.

Thanks to the plant hunters exploring new regions and introducing new species of plants, our palette of possibilities continues to expand. Plant breeders play their part, too, by producing longer-flowering or off-peak-

season cultivars and hybrids. This combination of factors adds up to us gardeners being able to get hold of unusual or relatively rare species which can extend the 'season' of our favourite plants. Once you're in the know and have stocked your patch with these season-extenders you'll be able to show off roses in spring or geraniums in late autumn. Expanding the seasons of particular plants not only means you get to grow more of the plants you love but also the ones that bring the possibility of extending surprising colours into more challenging months. So, if there's a particular genus you love, be it clematis or geraniums, it's possible to get more of that particular plant's qualities of form, longevity or colour for much, much longer.

GERANIUMS

FIRST INTO FLOWER

Most geraniums flower around early summer, with several continuing into autumn, but a few species bloom much earlier in the year. The shade-loving *Geranium phaeum* and its progeny *G.* × *monacense* are usually the first in flower in around mid-spring. Flower colours vary from violet to browns but I find the paler hues are most visible in shady settings. Blooms are small and down-turned with very prominent stamens. *G. phaeum* var. *phaeum* 'Samobor' is the classic, with dark purple-brown flowers and similar-coloured attractive leaf markings. *G. cinereum* comes later in spring and is a very different plant. It's super-short (15–20cm) with heavily veined petals in a range of pinks and needs a free-draining, gritty soil in full sun.

Geranium phaeum 'Advendo'
Foliage: mid-green
H/S 60cm × 70–80cm
Shape: well-formed bun
Position: shade
Soil: moisture-retentive but free-draining

PEAK SEASON

In early summer there is a convergence of geranium species which are too numerous to mention. So, I'm sticking to the ones I find most useful. *G. ibericum* is the soft, hairy-leafed plant I remember from my great-grandfather's cottage garden. It has dark violet flowers and a good domed form. *G. macrorrhizum* and its cultivars have distinctive deeply dissected leaves which make for great groundcover and autumn colour. Flowers are pink or white.

G. pratense has a delicate feel to its papery flowers in blues, pink and white with distinctive venation. *G. renardii* and *G. sanguineum* are also distinctly veined but are much shorter plants, at around 30cm. *G. renardii* has especially lovely textured leaves which look like finely cracked parched earth.

LAST IN FLOWER

Although the geraniums noted here start flowering in midsummer they are unrelenting flower factories which continue to bloom feverishly till mid-autumn. *G.* × *oxonianum* is perhaps best known, not least for its numerous cultivars in more than 50 shades of pink. Most flowers are a fairly standard geranium shape, but a few cultivars, such as *G.* × *oxonianum* f. *thurstanianum* 'Sherwood', have distinctive, dramatic, starry blooms. *G.* × *riversleaianum* forms give us two of the three longest-flowering geraniums. *G.* 'Mavis Simpson', discovered by a student in the Kew rock garden, is light pink and relentless from mid-summer to autumn. *G.* × r. 'Russell Prichard', in magenta, is similar in its enthusiasm. Finally, for midsummer to winter display, *G. wallichianum* cultivars, particularly the now famous *G.* Rozanne, are the business. Look out for *G.* 'Lilac Ice', a pale pink-violet sport of *G.* Rozanne which flowers for just as long!

Geranium 'Lilac Ice'
Foliage: mid-green, sometimes mottled
H/S 50cm × 1m
Shape: sprawling cloud
Position: full sun
Soil: moisture-retentive but free-draining

Top Geranium phaeum 'Advendo' blooms in spring.
Bottom Geranium 'Lilac Ice' flowers until late autumn.

Top Clematis erophylla 'Winter Beauty' blooms early/mid-winter. *Bottom Clematis armandii* 'Apple Blossom' opens in late winter.

FIRST INTO FLOWER

Clematis are so diverse that there's a plant in flower every month of year. The earliest to bloom are the evergreen forms which flower in late winter, such as *Clematis cirrhosa*, with their hellebore-looking pendulous flowers (see page 204) and *C. armandii*. These are classified as group 1 clematis and just need a tidy-up prune after flowering. Slightly further into spring, but still classed as group1 types, are *C. montana*, alpina and macropetala. All have small but vibrantly coloured flowers. *C. montana* cultivars are mostly mid-pink and rampant, while the bell-shaped flowers of *C. alpina* are violet-blue and the cultivars of *C. macropetala* pale pinks, mauves and blues.

Clematis armandii 'Apple Blossom'
Foliage: Dark, ribbed, glossy
H/S 5-6m x 5m+
Shape: rampant tendrilled climber
Position: sun to part-shade (a west wall is good)
Soil: woodsy and moisture-retentive

PEAK SEASON

Very late spring and early summer sees possibly the biggest range of clematis in bloom. These are the large-flowered cultivars such as the huge double-flowered, light violet *C.* 'Vyvyan Pennell'. Other well-known forms include *C. florida* 'Sieboldii', which is white with a striking boss of purple stamens. They are all classified as group 2 clematis, meaning they need pruning back to strong buds in early spring. Other notable cultivars include the 15cm-wide *C.* 'Doctor Ruppel'. It's flowers are dark pink with white bleeding in from the edge of its petals.

LAST INTO FLOWER

Late summer till late autumn sees lots of what I think of as the best clematis – often smaller flowered than the mid-summer types but all the more elegant for it. Falling into the group 3 category, these plants encompass a wide range of forms. Viticellas have fine foliage and stems festooned with small-to-medium flowers. Delicious notable cultivars are *C.* 'etoile Violette', with nearly round flowers in a dark pink-violet, and the white, pale green and pale violet *C.* 'Alba Luxurians'. Other late-season lovelies include *C. tangutica*, with its yellow, bell-shaped, thick-petalled flowers which look as lovely in bud as they do open, and *C. texensis*, with its mainly red tulip-shaped flowers. All will bloom well into autumn, ready to greet the first of the winter clematis such as the white bell-shaped *C. urophylla* 'Winter Beauty'. Prune all the group 3 plants in early spring, removing all foliage and stems to 30cm from the ground.

Clematis texensis 'Princess Diana'
Foliage: mid green and smallish
H/S 3m x 3m
Shape: delicate climber
Position: sun to part-shade
Soil: woodsy and moisture-retentive

TULIPS

FIRST INTO FLOWER

The first tulips to bloom in late winter/early spring are usually the short-stemmed wild species, *Tulipa kaufmanniana* types and the equally short *T. greigii* hybrids. All three types have presumably evolved to stay low and nestled within their leaves to avoid icy blasts from late-winter weather. Many of the wild species and *T. kaufmanniana* types have small star-shaped flowers in myriad colours, while the *T. greigii* types are true red or strong yellow, often with leaves patterned in a purple-brown grid.

Tulipa polychroma

Foliage: grey-green
H/S 15cm × 10cm
Shape: multi-headed star-shaped blooms
Position: full sun
Soil: sharp-draining but moisture-retentive

PEAK SEASON

A large proportion of tulips appear around mid-spring and encompass many forms, shapes and sizes. Early single/double tulips, as they are known, are often the first peak-season types to flower. They have mainly ovoid blooms in virtually every colour on stems averaging 30cm high. Other useful types at this time of year include the mainly yellow and red *T. fosterianas* and the Darwin forms. I find these especially useful

and long-lasting, both in flower and year to year. They average 60cm high and include the dreamy light pink-apricot *T.* 'Daydream' and pale buttermilk-yellow *T.* 'Ivory Floradale'. Also in full bloom at this time are the mid-season tulips including the sumptuous *T.* 'Abu Hassan'. Its dark purple-brown flowers, which are trimmed with yellow-brown, sound ugly in print but are absolutely breathtaking when they are in front of you.

LAST INTO FLOWER

Come late spring, the single and double 'late' forms such as the self-described *T.* 'Violet Beauty' and pale-pink *T.* 'Angélique' are blooming. These are accompanied by the *T. viridiflora* forms which come in most colours accompanied by stripes of green, and the Rembrandts, with petals decorated in flame patterns. The tall-stemmed lily-flowered types, such as the classic yellow, pointy-petalled *T.* 'West Point', are also in full swing, along with feather-petalled parrot forms in most shades you care to think of.

Tulipa 'Black Parrot'

Foliage: grey-green
H/S 60cm × 10cm
Shape: ovoid and feathered
Position: full sun
Soil: sharp-draining but moisture-retentive

Top **Tulipa polychroma** is the first to brave late winter.
Bottom **Tulipa** 'Black Parrot' holds on till late spring.

NARCISSUS

Top *Narcissus* 'Rijnveld's Early Sensation' is usually the first daff of the year. *Bottom Narcissus* 'Cedric Morris' appears in autumn.

FIRST INTO FLOWER

From late winter onwards the first narcissus of the new year appear. Short, delicate, wild species such as the translucent white *Narcissus cantabricus* sometimes put in the first showing, but this is dependent on a very sheltered site or cold glasshouse. It is a similar story with *N. tazetta* types (similar to paperwhites). The *N. cyclamineus* clan, however, are hardy. These plucky little daffs are great for late-winter/early spring display. *N.* 'Snipe', with its typical short habit, long corolla and swept-back petals, is especially early, along with the squat mid-yellow *N. minor* and *N. × odorus*. A few other random forms, often with February in their title, muster early flowering, along with dwarf hybrids such as the classic *N.* 'Tête-à-Tête'.

Narcissus 'Rijnveld's Early Sensation' (late winter)

Foliage: Mid-green
H/S 45cm
Shape: typical trumpet
Position: full sun to light shade
Soil: moisture-retentive with reasonable drainage

PEAK SEASON

Mid-spring sees the bulk of narcissus come into bloom. The classic trumpet forms with a long wide corolla (trumpet section) such as the orange-yellow *N.* 'Dutch Master' lead the way here – they're the types you expect to see in public parks and gardens. Also, during this peak time the large- and small-cupped forms are open. These are distinctive for their short corolla and include delights such as *N.* 'Faith', with its peachy trumpet and rounded white petals. The doubles are also doing their thing come mid-spring. These include notable forms such as *N.* 'Sir Winston Churchill', with its mashed-up yolky centre of yellow-orange trimmed with white petals.

LAST INTO FLOWER

For late-spring and occasionally early-summer flowering we turn to the *T. triandrus, jonquilla* and *poeticus* types. And for truly late-flowering (or early flowering, depending on how you look at it) there's the joy of *N.* 'Cedric Morris', which flowers in late autumn. *T. triandrus* types have a delicate elegance with multiple down-turned heads on each of their stems. A good form is *N.* 'Hawera', with its well-spaced, soft-yellow, starry flowers. The *T. jonquilla* types have a similar look but with shorter corollas and often a good scent. Try *N.* 'Pipit' for its pale yellow, white-striped flowers.

My favourite daffs of the lot are *N. poeticus* forms (opposite). These have wide flat-faced flowers (often white) with short, small corollas. They are loaded with scent heady enough to carry across the garden. *N. poeticus* var. *recurvus* is stunning with its white, scented blooms centred with tiny red, yellow and green corollas. It will flower from late spring into summer during cooler years.

Narcissus 'Cedric Morris' (late autumn)

Foliage: mid grey-green
H/S 30cm
Shape: long trumpet with forward-pointing petals
Position: full sun to part-shade
Soil: most with some moisture-retention

ROSES

FIRST INTO FLOWER

Few roses dare to brave spring flowering, most wait till early summer, but among those that do there are some real beauties. The famed climber *Rosa banksiae* 'Lutea', which needs a really warm wall, produces an abundance of small pale yellow flowers in late spring. Also eager to bloom are the flower carpet groundcover roses (white and pink are best). For larger shrubby specimens, *R.* 'Mortimer Sackler', an English rose, has smallish pink flowers that arrive in late spring and go on virtually all year. For a wilder look, *R. pimpinellifolia* can also flower very early with small, single, white flowers followed by delicious mahogany-coloured glossy berries in late summer and autumn. Earliest of all roses is *R. xanthina* 'Canary Bird'.

Rosa xanthina 'Canary Bird'

Foliage: evergreen, light green, ferny.
H/S 2m x 2m
Shape: columnar/freeform
Position: full sun
Soil: rich and free-draining but moisture-retentive

PEAK SEASON

Roses can be broadly broken into two groups – old and modern. Many of the old roses only flower once while lots of their modern cousins can bloom perpetually or repeat-flower several times in a season. For this reason I mainly focus on the modern types, especially the English roses developed by David Austin – the diverse parentage of these plants means they often have an old rose look and scent but with the repeat-flowering qualities of modern roses. Peak season, in early summer, sees the vast majority of roses at their zenith. Hybrid tea roses, perhaps the most commonly seen in gardens, produce pointy (or high-centred) roses in every conceivable colour except blue. Floribundas are similar but produce clusters of smaller flowers. Both bloom until mid-autumn. Modern climbers have a similar form and colour range. The classy light pink climber *R.* 'New Dawn' flowers till autumn, but several other climbers only flower once. Groundcover roses are also highly floriferous, blooming from spring till winter with minimal input required.

LAST INTO FLOWER

As winter creeps up on the garden certain roses are able to carry their colour until the frosts. Those that flowered their hearts out in summer, such as the hybrid teas, floribundas, climbers and groundcover roses (flower carpet) will keep blooming, especially with the assistance of deadheading and regular feeds. This means it's possible to sustain just about any colour (except blue) into autumn. Other cultivars, such as *R.* 'Ballerina', which have gently thrown out flowering spurs since summer, also continue to do so. Given good weather, many of the English roses continue to perform. *R.* The Mayflower, which starts flowering in late spring, will go on till early winter along with the delicious pink *R.* 'Mortimer Sackler'.

Rosa Molineux

Foliage: mid-green, glossy
H/S 1m x 1m
Shape: ball
Position: full sun
Soil: enriched and moisture-retentive

Top Rosa 'Molineux' is amongst roses which flower into winter. *Bottom Rosa* xanthina 'Canary Bird' is the first in spring.

PERFECT
PAIRS

PERFECT PLANT PARTNERS

Like strawberries and cream, certain plants just go together. Whether it's due to dreamy colour associations, similar flowering seasons, successional colour or simply support for one another, these plants pack more punch in pairs. Cynaras can look tired by the end of summer, but with an ipomoea scrambling through its stems the plant takes on new life and a new role, not as star turn but as a support structure. Lily-of-the-valley is all but frazzled by late summer, but inter-planted with autumn cyclamen, a new patch of flowers and marbled foliage carries the planting through winter and into spring, when the lily-of-the-valley returns. These happy partnerships of supportive couples are a simple way of adding more colour to the 365-day garden, even if space is tight. Most are very simple to create from scratch, or why not try playing garden matchmaker and introduce a new plant to one already established in the garden? There are thousands of possible pairs, so finding a love-match is a fun process to experiment with, but if you find tried-and-tested pairs more reassuring, all these plant combinations are guaranteed to work.

For... wilder gardens

Erigeron karvinskianus with *Campanula poscharskyana*

This magical pairing is sometimes created by chance. Both these plants are free-spirited and often seed and establish in unintended places. Their favoured spots tend to be dry-stone walls, rockeries, paving gaps and other appealing crevices. There's a street in London whose low walls I've seen become slowly and beautifully colonised by the twosome. Both flower through late spring and into summer, but the erigeron will carry on till the frosts. They can be scattered as seeds but a safer bet is establishing a few 'mother' plants of both species and letting nature do its thing.

For... glorious autumn display

Salvia guaranitica with *Ipomoea lobata* growing up it

Yellow-orange and blue-violet are contrasting colours, so their coupling makes both of them glow that little bit more. This pair of plants also carries several other colours close to orange and blue, creating an exciting confection of hues. Well, I love it. To make this late summer and autumn pairing work the salvia needs to be left unpruned over winter. This way it provides a woody climbing frame early on. The ipomoea needs starting under glass and growing up a cane to aid its initial adventures into the salvia's branches. Both appreciate a liquid feed as they develop over summer.

> *Because they are contrasting colours, their coupling makes both of them glow that little bit more.*

For... brightness in dappled shade

Astrantia major with *Euphorbia griffithii* 'Fireglow'

This perfect late-spring combination is growing at The Garden House, in Devon. It feels like a happy union of two plants that are not just growing side by side but are intermeshed with each other. Long before the astrantia has made a decent hummock of leaves, the euphorbia grabs all the light it needs as its urgent stems emerge in glorious Technicolor. Short at first, these stems stretch up to match the astrantia through late spring into midsummer with its leaves and bracts graduating through various complimentary shades before they disappear. Both appreciate slightly damper conditions and work best in speckled shade.

For... successional colour

Cynara cardunculus with *Ipomoea purpurea*

This pair doubles up on flower power without taking any additional ground space – perfect for smaller gardens. While the silver-leafed cynara sends flower stems skyward in midsummer, the ipomoea is not far behind, twining itself some 2 metres up its willing supporter's shoots. Come late summer the partnership flourishes as the muted lilac-blue flowers of the cynara open to jostle with the subtle magenta trumpets of the ipomoea. The cynara may only stretch to six weeks of flower but the ipomoea keeps blooming among its willing partner's stems till the onset of autumn.

" This pair doubles up on flower power without taking any additional ground space – perfect for smaller gardens. "

For... colour, texture and colonisation

Verbascum 'Pink Petticoats' with *Foeniculum vulgare* 'Purpureum'

I've used this planting combination time and again for its delicate subtlety. Both plants need blazing sunshine to thrive, so they shouldn't be packed together like flower show border-fillers, but given space in a free-draining bed where they can be planted in a few repeated layers to enhance their meadowy pairing. The verbascum's dark buds are picked out by the burgundy filigree leaves of the fennel. This combination changes as the verbascum opens to reveal pale pink flowers providing a delicate counterpoint. Another verbascum, new to gardens, *V. phoeniceum* 'Rosetta', would couple up well with the fennel, too. It has the added advantage of self-seeding in its immediate locale, giving rise, along with the self-seeding fennel, to a gently expanding garden partnership.

For…year-round display in a small space

Convallaria majalis with Cyclamen hederifolium

By sharing the same patch of ground, lily-of-the-valley and ivy-leaved cyclamen have all seasons covered. Not only do they bloom five months apart but they also do a great job of disguising each other's less-appealing traits. As the leaves of the cyclamen fade in spring, so the shoots and flowers of the lily-of-the-valley push through and cover them. Come September, as the leaves of the lily-of-the-valley start to show the scars of summer, so the flowers of the cyclamen appear, shortly followed by the leaves, keeping the patch fresh and well-furnished through to the following spring, when the baton is handed back.

For... spring zing

Tulipa 'Spring Green' with Polystichum setiferum (Divisilobum Group)

This simple pairing peaks in late spring with a freshness and purity usually reserved for earlier in the year. As the lacy fern fronds unfurl, all soft and delicate, the tulip pushes dusty blue-green leaves and buds from below ground. The resulting partnership of greens and the contrast between the bold tulip leaf and fine fern are this pair's first act, but the finale is yet to come. Once the fern fronds are fully opened to reveal pale green leaves and orange-brown leaf stems, they lay in wait for the tulip. The moment of glory finally (well, about three weeks' later) arrives as the tulip opens to reveal its whiter-than-white petals streaked with panels of the freshest green. Grow them in light shade on a moisture-retentive but free-draining soil. For full effect, go for 6–7 tulips per fern in the planting.

> **These super-sized perennials give the feeling of a fantasy meadow – all delicate, pristine and alluring.**

For... making the most of one space

Nerine bowdenii with Iris (bearded)

Both these plants flower spectacularly for short windows but look pretty dull for the rest of the year. This can be countered by interplanting the two together. As the iris flowers fade in late spring, so the nerine starts putting up its foliage, which keeps the planting looking fresh through summer. Spacing is important here; the nerines need to be close enough to work as a pair with the iris, but not so close that they smother or shade its rhizomes. As autumn arrives the nerine brings the planting fully back to life with its electric-pink flowers. It's even possible to slot another season of colour in and dot winter-flowering *Iris reticulata* between the rhizomes of the bearded ones.

For... striking summer contrast

Erigeron 'Darkest of All' with Milium effusum

Five years after planting this combination in a Norfolk garden, it was great to return and see it thriving. It could have gone horribly wrong, like some of the violet and yellow experiments I've tried. This feels about right. Both colours are bright and saturated; they peak together and the matching yellow of the grass and the erigeron's disk centre help things along. To keep the planting in check the seedlings of the milium need regular removal so they don't grow up and smother the erigeron. Both thrive in full sun on a moisture-retentive but free-draining soil.

For... supporting pollinators

Veronicastrum virginicum with Foeniculum vulgare

Pairing the gentle colours and soft textures of these two lofty perennials gives the feeling of a super-sized fantasy meadow – all delicate, pristine and alluring. In truth, they're both pretty tough perennials that will stand up to a summer of wind and rain better than your average meadow. They are both fairly slow to establish, but after three years or so they have formed into substantial stands. Their flowers' muted versions of violet and yellow gently contrast but maintain an understated look. Grow them in full sun on a free-draining soil where they'll be festooned with pollinators through mid- and late summer. Both maintain attractive exoskeletons in winter which provide homes to beneficial lacewings and hoverflies.

For... intense colour

Alchemilla mollis with *Geranium psilostemon*

I use this pairing for its shameless intensity. The combination of purple-red and light yellow-green may be the stuff of kids' sweet wrappers but in summer it's just the ticket to keep things fresh. Both plants emerge at a similar point in spring and both can be sheared over after flowering. This way the alchemilla will produce a fresh crop of leaves and the geranium will flower again. The pairing is not as exciting second time around, but to have fresh foliage and flowers in late summer and autumn is a boon. Use the pair as border-fronters or in a gravel garden.

For... long-term colour on walls

Clematis 'Perle d'Azur' with *Rosa* 'New Dawn'

Pairing climbing roses and clematis is not revolutionary, but it can be a battle to pick partners with a balanced degree of vigour and flowering so that they won't overwhelm one another. Two plants that can live in peace, and which were recommended by Gertrude Jekyll, are the powder-puff-pink *Rosa* 'New Dawn' and delicately translucent, blue *Clematis* 'Perle d' Azur'. Grown on a pergola or relatively sunny wall, they'll paint a romantic picture through summer, peaking in July. After that, the clematis slows its flowering, but I've known the rose to keep popping buds till late autumn.

For… a striking colour combination mid-border

Achillea 'Terracotta' with Aconitum carmichaelii (Wilsonii Group)

Combining flower hues from opposite sides of the colour wheel guarantees vibrant contrasts that cry out for attention. This visually compelling pair work best en masse in herbaceous borders, where their flowering overlaps for several weeks in late summer. The aconite tends to finish flowering first but the achillea can continue for some time, often creating a secondary colour combination when its dusty orange flowers are set against the yellow autumn leaves of the aconite. Give the pair a backdrop of silver foliage and their colours radiate with even more zing. Aconites tend to prefer slightly moister sites than achilleas, but with the addition of good garden compost at planting time both will be content.

For... easy successional planting

Hyacinthoides non-scripta with *Aster divaricatus*

Here one plant hides the sins of another while sharing the same spot. In late spring bluebells are resplendent with their wonderful near violet-blue flowers, but as these fade and the foliage senesces to yellow, ugliness creeps in. At, or just before this moment the aster launches into growth with its sprawling, nearly black, groundcovering stems which quickly hide the bluebell remains. The aster rapidly bulks out ready for midsummer, when it produces a galaxy of tiny white stars like a froth across its surface. An autumn cut back of the aster will see the ground ready for the emerging bluebells the following year.

> ❝ *Together this power couple will keep churning out blooms from early summer to autumn. Long-term loveliness.* ❞

For... classic companionship

Rosa 'Dusky Maiden' with *Geranium* 'Brookside'

For generations gardeners have relied on the comfortable pairing of roses and geraniums. Often they are selected to flower together in early summer, but those plants which continue to flower beyond this are a bonus. The dark purple-red flowers of *Rosa* 'Dusky Maiden' glow in sunlight and are further intensified by the pale blue petals of *Geranium* 'Brookside'. This pair share a magic early summer moment together, but for a similar-coloured longer-term pairing try growing repeat-flowering *Rosa* Munstead Wood and *Geranium* Rozanne. Together this power couple will keep churning out blooms from early summer to autumn. Long-term loveliness.

For... a subtle summer-long pairing

Nicotiana mutabilis with *Verbena bonariensis*

I'd love to say I created this subtle pairing after much thought and consideration, but in truth it happened quite by accident. While planting a patch of nicotiana, to follow on from a clump of peonies, I churned up the soil enough to cause the germination of verbena seeds which were dormant below the surface. The resultant pairing matches in height and colour intensity while at the same time they both retain their lofty, see-through appeal. Grown together the verbena will continue to self-seed, if it's on an open free-draining soil, while the nicotiana needs growing under glass (or on a windowsill) each year. As a pair, they'll bloom in unison from midsummer till mid-autumn (about four months). A third, much earlier, layer can be slotted into the planting with the addition of late tulips such as *Tulipa* 'Black Parrot', which will re-bloom every year given a relatively free-draining soil.

AUTUMN PLANTS

EARLY AUTUMN

Agastache
'Firebird'

Though this tender perennial looks very salvia-like, it's blessed with a colour combo that its horticultural cousin can't match. From midsummer to mid-autumn it is smothered in vibrant orange flowers which are intensified by a grey hint to the leaves. It's compact enough for container growing but is best shown off in groups, where it sits with equal ease among summer bedding or herbaceous plantings. Even on well-drained soils there is no guarantee it will withstand winter, so it is best brought into a cool glasshouse, or you can take cuttings in late summer. Full sun is essential for it to fully develop its striking orange/grey pairing.

H/S 70cm × 40cm
Season of colour: Fls: summer–autumn; Fol: spring–autumn
Colour combination: violet/purple/blue/red/light yellow
Grow it with: *Kniphofia* 'Nancy's Red' and *Elymus arenarius*
Follow-on plant: dwarf species tulips (planted as the agastache is lifted)

Eucryphia × nymansensis
'Nymansay'

Come early autumn most shrubs and trees have finished flowering, but not eucryphia. This cultivar, a hybrid between two Chilean species, has white flowers which fall somewhere between a hellebore and a philadelphus and glow with the freshness of spring. Liberally decorated with blooms, this evergreen tree (or very big shrub) has a columnar habit but is virtually unseen in summer due to its dark-green leaves. It's an acid lover, but the specimen I know best is at least 30 years old with roots which extend well beyond the peat bed it was first planted into – so there is a degree of lime tolerance. Choose a sunny site, acidify the soil with the addition of a peat-free alternative, stake well on the windward side and enjoy.

H/S 12m × 5m
Season of colour: Fls: autumn; Fol: year-round
Colour combination: yellow/purple/pink/white
Grow it with: *Anemone × hybrida* 'Honorine Jobert'
Follow-on plant: *Clematis* 'Bill MacKenzie'

Aconitum carmichaelii (Arendsii Group) 'Arendsii'

Early autumn is often awash with flame colours, so the rich violet-blue of this columnar aconite makes for a perfect counterpoint. Blooms are hooded and not well defined at a distance but provide ample spikes of colour which ignite oranges and reds. Given the right season its finely divided leaves can develop a striking yellow tone later on, contrasting well with parched grass stems and reds. Grow it in a woodsy soil in full sun or dappled shade. Try it mid-border or as a succession plant to follow hellebores or other woodland edgers. It's poisonous, so glove-up when you're dealing with it.

H/S 1.2m × 50cm
Season of colour: Fls: autumn; Fol: spring–autumn
Colour combination: yellow/red/orange/orange-brown/light yellow
Grow it with: *Imperata cylindrica* 'Red Baron'
Follow-on plant: *Viburnum opulus* (as a backdrop)

Sedum 'Cauli'

Sedums are a garden must for me. Most are doing something 365 days a year, be it beautiful buds, flowers, foliage, dried seed heads or emerging stems. Cultivars of S. *spectabile* tend to have larger domed heads, while S. *telephium* cultivars form smaller flower clusters. S. 'Red Cauli' is truly special; it has multi-tonal leaves with hints of purple, blue and mid-green, while stems are a dark purple. These subtle colours, combined with dark pink-red flowers on a compact domed plant, make this sedum irresistible. Grow in it full sun and avoid excess water and nutrients as these can cause it to over-extend, flop and lose its colour intensity. Chopping it back by half in late spring will delay flowering and increase the number of blooms.

H/S 45cm × 45cm
Season of colour: Fls: summer–autumn; Fol: spring–autumn
Colour combination: silver/violet/green/grey-blue/purple
Grow it with: *Aster* 'Purple Dome'
Follow-on plant: *Pennisetum villosum*

Rudbeckia var. *sullivantii* 'Goldsturm'

A favourite among proponents of the 'new wave' planting style that emerged in the 1990s, this daisy is ubiquitous but none the less desirable. The sheer volume of yellow flowers from summer through autumn could look brash but the black cones in their centres stud the sea of yellow and break its intensity. Maybe it's because it is from the US prairies, or because it is so commonly planted with grasses that this easy association somehow seems right. Plant it en masse but balance its blocky growth with feathery plants and those in the violet range. Choose a sunny position in soil that is moisture-retentive but free-draining. Split and divide in spring as required.

H/S 70cm × 70cm
Season of colour: Fls: summer–autumn; Fol: spring–autumn
Colour combination: violet/green/orange/orange-brown
Grow it with: *Stipa gigantea*
Follow-on plant: *Leucojum vernum*

Anemone hupehensis var. *japonica* 'Pamina'

There are anemones for virtually every season and late summer belongs to the Japanese ones. *A. hupehensis* waits summer-long before presenting a jostling crowd of red-pink double flowers perched on willowy wands. In the wild it favours a moisture-retentive, woodland-edge environment but will tolerate full sun to dappled shade in the garden. Its unassuming hummock of foliage provides good groundcover through summer and does not need staking. It can be split as required in spring. *A. hybrida* 'Honorine Jobert' is equally, if not more, desirable. Its radiant white blooms, backed by the dark foliage of another plant or a woodland, are delicious.

H/S 70cm × 45cm
Season of colour: Fls: summer–autumn; Fol: spring–autumn
Colour combination: violet/green/orange/orange-brown
Grow it with: *Aster × frikartii* 'Mönch'
Follow-on plant: *Allium neapolitanum* Cowanii Group

Tritonia disticha subsp. rubrolucens

Pale pink is so often the colour of early summer, but tritonia extends that feel-good pastel palette into autumn. Once classified as a pink crocosmia, this corm now has its very own name. It makes a light tuft of fine leaves and slim flower stems that all but disappear at a distance, giving the impression of floating flowers. Individual blooms are a light red-pink with subtle darker venation and a little yellow blotch. It feels like a frail wild flower, all willowy and wispy, but will form reasonable clumps over several years. I've failed to establish it in the past but now rely on a good dose of organic matter and grit at planting to ensure good nutrition and free drainage (especially over winter when it can rot off).

H/S 60cm × 40cm
Season of colour: Fls: summer–autumn; Fol: spring–autumn
Colour combination: violet/green/grey-blue/pale blue
Grow it with: *Artemisia* 'Powis Castle'
Follow-on plant: *Tulipa clusiana*

10
MORE EARLY AUTUMN PLANTS

1. *Pennisetum setaceum 'Rubrum'*
2. *Persicaria amplexicaulis 'Firetail'*
3. *Liriope muscari*
4. *Clerodendrum trichotomum*
5. *Ceratostigma willmottianum*
6. *Dianella tasmanica*
7. *Cyclamen hederifolium*
8. *Rosa 'Mortimer Sackler'*
9. *Ipomoea lobata*
10. *Vernonia crinita*

Kniphofia 'Creamsicle'

Picking the perfect poker used to be a choice between early and late-flowering species, or the occasional repeat-bloomer, but US breeding has changed that. *K.* 'Creamsicle' flowers all the way through summer into autumn. Ok, it has a silly name, but its compact form, fine leaves and succession of light orange to orange-red flowers more than make up for it. Try growing it with purple trailing verbenas in a pot, with silver as a backdrop or to provide the colour bridge between red and yellow autumn flowers. Give it a free-draining soil in blazing sun and be sure to deadhead.

H/S 60cm × 60cm
Season of colour: Fls: summer–autumn; Fol: nearly year round
Colour combination: purple/violet/grey-blue/pale blue/yellow-green
Grow it with: *Verbena* 'Sunvop'
Follow-on plant: *Milium effusum* 'Aureum'

Tricyrtis 'Empress'

The shady forests of Taiwan are home to several toad lilies whose common name, evocative as it is, is thought to have derived from a modern myth involving luring edible toads with the flower's scent! *T.* 'Empress' is a striking sight in humus-rich, shady conditions where its white flowers blotched with hundreds of purple dots glow out of the darkness. It requires little attention so long as the conditions are right and will slowly form a stocky colony. Flowering can extend to two months, bringing life into woodland areas whose spring and summer display have long since faded. The plant hunters at Crug Farm, in Wales, continue to discover and introduce new forms of this beguiling plant.

H/S 80cm × 60cm
Season of colour: Fls: summer–autumn; Fol: late spring–autumn
Colour combination: white/green/purple/pink
Grow it with: *Anemone hupehensis* var. *japonica* 'Pamina'
Follow-on plant: *Anemone nemorosa*

Gladiolus murielae

Looking like a series of crisply folded origami birds, the flowers of this exceptional white and purple perennial gladioli bring a unique freshness to autumn plantings. They form a fine stand when grown en masse but I prefer them scattered between shorter, well-behaved perennials. Flowering can last several months as a succession of blooms appear on the ever-extending flower stems. Plant their corms in spring on a free-draining soil in full sun, preferably close to a path or window, where their addictively heady scent is within sniffing distance. The perfume really cranks up in the evening and the flowers become luminescent in low light, making it a perfect plant for the night garden.

H/S 90cm × 10cm
Season of colour: Fls: autumn; Fol: late spring–autumn
Colour combination: green/purple/silver/blue
Grow it with: *Succisa pratensis*
Follow-on plant: *Allium* sp.

Leonotis leonurus

This South African plant has to be one of the tallest and most dramatic annuals. From seed sown in mid-spring it's capable of reaching heights of 2.5 metres before the frost puts pay to its exuberant ways. It's often in flower by midsummer but it is not until mid-autumn that it peaks, with whorls of dark orange felty flowers arranged up the stem. Its columnar form can hold its own but a few bamboo cane supports won't go a miss in exposed areas. Plant it with other late-season doers such as dahlias and cannas in a moisture-retentive but free-draining soil in as much sun as you can muster.

H/S 2m × 1m
Season of colour: Fls: summer–autumn; Fol: summer–autumn
Colour combination: violet/blue/red/blue-grey/yellow-green/white
Grow it with: *Arundo donax* var. *versicolor*
Follow-on plant: *Erysimum* 'Bowles's Mauve'

MID-AUTUMN

Helianthus
'Lemon Queen'

The 'fresh as a daisy' cliché should be reserved for this American perennial. It takes most of the year to reach flowering height, then just as all else is about to hibernate for winter its pale yellow flowers emerge. These blooms appear on the top of the 1.8-metre stems, so it needs a spot at the back of the border. Despite this its sheer volume of light yellow flowers, set off with black stamens, can't be missed. It's tolerant of most soils (I've grown it all over the place) but does best on a moisture-retentive but free-draining soil in full sun. Flowering can sometimes come early, but whenever it starts the plant will summon up 6–7 weeks of daisy freshness.

H/S 2.2m × 1m+
Season of colour: Fls: late summer–autumn; Fol: spring–autumn
Colour combination: violet/blue/green/yellow/dark purple-brown
Grow it with: *Aster novae-angliae* 'Barr's Violet'
Follow-on plant: *Narcissus* spp. around its base

Salvia
'Purple Majesty'

Striking as it is, without a supporting cast this salvia's star won't shine. Its flowers are a rich, velvety violet-blue – so dark that inky background foliage and shadows can drink it up, but when paired with sepia-toned grasses or an orange dahlia it is enlivened. Lighting is important, too, and autumn provides just the right golden tone and low angle. This salvia is probably best described as a woody perennial. It retains a defoliated shrubby structure over winter, which, if protected and not cut back by more than half, will see flowers appearing by midsummer. Grow it in full sun on a rich but free-draining soil and take a few late-summer cuttings in case there is a breach in the winter protection.

H/S 2m × 1.5m
Season of colour: Fls: late summer–autumn; Fol: spring–autumn
Colour combination: orange/orange-brown/dark pink/red/light green
Grow it with: *Ipomoea lobata*
Follow-on plant: *Iris foetidissima* (its orange seeds also contrast later in the year)

Rosa glauca

It's hard to pick a favourite summer rose, but of those that shine in autumn this one is difficult to beat. True, its flowers are so-so, but the foliage and hips are magic. Try it in mixed or herbaceous borders where the fine, pale blue leaves, edged with a hint of red, and the heavy pendulous bunches of hips act initially as supporting cast in summer then rise to stardom in autumn. Like many of the species roses it's blissfully disease-free. Grow this rose in full sun or dappled shade (the leaves won't be as blue here) in an enriched soil. Pruning is restricted to removing ugly or badly placed branches, otherwise the plant looks after itself.

H/S 2m × 1.5m
Season of colour: Fls: early summer; Fol: spring–autumn
Colour combination: orange/red/white/dark pink/violet
Grow it with: *Rhus typhina* 'Dissecta'
Follow-on plant: *Nonea lutea* (allowed to self-seed in its vicinity)

Lobelia tupa

This is the Duracell bunny of plants. It can come into bloom as early as midsummer and just keeps going until early winter. Its lofty flowering stems can reach 2 metres or more, with at least 1 metre of the height in gone-over flower stems as the blooms appear ever higher. This is not a plant for the fainthearted, it's very poisonous and to get the full effect you need to plant a minimum of five in a group, preferably ten. This way, their exotic flowers form a screen of true red. Grow it mid-border with pale blue, buff or grey foliage behind it to intensify its colour. Best in full sun on moisture-retentive but free-draining soils.

H/S 2m × 70cm
Season of colour: Fls: summer–autumn; Fol: spring–autumn
Colour combination: orange/violet/purple/yellow-green/pale green
Grow it with: *Leonotis leonurus*
Follow-on plant: Alliums (will bloom higher than the emerging lobelia foliage in spring)

Chrysanthemum 'Mary Stoker'

I fell in love with the musty scent and intense velvety colours of chrysanthemums in my mother's polytunnel as an 8-year-old. C. 'Mary Stoker' certainly has the scent but the flowers are a slightly more subtle apricot (pink-orange) single daisy. They are also one of the few chrysanthemums truly suited to garden growing. C. 'Mei-Kyo' (pale pink) and C. 'Robin' (orange) are the other two I find useful in the border, but they are a bit dense and blocky compared to C. 'Mary Stoker'. She has an open, slightly straggly even, form with every stem concluding in an apricot bloom which is just crying out for a hoar-frost makeover.

H/S 70cm × 70cm
Season of colour: Fls: summer–autumn; Fol: spring–autumn
Colour combination: orange/violet/purple/yellow-green/pale green
Grow it with: *Symphyotrichum novi-belgii* 'Purple Dome'
Follow-on plant: *Ipheion uniflorum* 'Wisley Blue'

Aster amellus 'Veilchenkönigin'

This aster looks positively regal with its sumptuous blue-violet flowers, so it comes as no surprise that its name translates as 'Violet Queen'. Through late summer and into autumn (around four months) it displays a succession of rich, delicious blooms which look especially dramatic against the senescing yellow leaves of autumn. Like the other *Aster amellus* cultivars, it is mildew-free and holds its form well against the rains, winds and hoar frosts of autumn. Pair it with grasses and yellow daisies to intensify its colour. Splitting and dividing in spring every few years will keep the patch fresh and prevent the centre dying out. Choose a spot in full sun on a moisture-retentive but free-draining soil.

H/S 50cm × 60cm
Season of colour: Fls: late summer–autumn; Fol: spring–autumn
Colour combination: orange/yellow/red/purple/white/green/silver
Grow it with: *Kniphofia* 'Luna'
Follow-on plant: *Allium* sp.

Rudbeckia triloba

Gardens may be awash with yellow daisies in autumn but this small-flowered wild species stands out thanks to its petite, rounded petals and large dark brown central cones. It has a columnar habit with flowers scattered through its upper reaches and needs replacing every few years, as it's short-lived. This is most easily achieved by collecting and drying seed in autumn and sowing it in early spring the following year. Rudbeckia hails from the American prairies, meaning it's quite a sociable creature that will happily sidle up to tall grasses and wispy perennials. It will bloom relentlessly from late summer till the onset of winter.

H/S 1m × 60cm
Season of colour: Fls: summer–late autumn; Fol: spring–autumn
Colour combination: orange/violet/purple/red/pale green
Grow it with: *Panicum virgatum* 'Heavy Metal'
Follow-on plant: *Smyrnium perfoliatum*

Nerine bowdenii

South Africa provides gardeners with a wealth of colour-rich bulbous plants including gladiolus and amaryllis, but few can match the elegance of delicate nerines. Breeding has led to an array of cultivars from the most timid pink through some peachy shades to darkest pink. Despite all these offerings, the wild species still steals the show for me. For around 4–6 weeks in autumn nothing in the garden can compete with its jaw-dropping, neon-pink flowers. Nerines thrive on tough love, so are best grown on well-drained gritty soil with their bulbs protruding slightly above the soil surface – think of them like bearded iris. Don't be tempted to split them up too often, they flower better when their bulbs are congested.

H/S 60cm × 10cm
Season of colour: Fls: autumn; Fol: spring–autumn
Colour combination: orange/violet/purple/pale green/dark pink/light violet
Grow it with: *Aster amellus* 'Veilchenkönigin'
Follow-on plant: *Iris germanica*

Hesperantha coccinea 'Major'

Autumn conjures up images of fiery reds, oranges and yellows, but these hues are often the result of senescing leaves and tend to be a little muted. This is where this kaffir lily comes into its own – its flowers are red, very red, and glossy. I've tried a few cultivars over the years but always return to *H. coccinea* 'Major' as it manages to flower from late summer till late autumn and can even offer up bonus flower spikes at other times. It's virtually evergreen and thrives in damp soils but mustn't sit wet over winter, so a heavy mulch is required. Flower stems can become a little flailing but light, supportive pea sticks in late spring redress this.

H/S 60cm × 60cm
Season of colour: Fls: summer–late autumn; Fol: virtually year-round
Colour combination: violet/blue/orange/light green/light blue/blue
Grow it with: *Hosta sieboldiana* var. *elegans*
Follow-on plant: *Leucojum vernum*

10
MORE
MID-AUTUMN
PLANTS

1 *Lespedeza thunbergii*

2 *Plectranthus argentatus*

3 *Hydrangea paniculata*

4 *Begonia 'Benitochiba'*

5 *Aster lateriflorus* var. *horizontalis*

6 *Dahlia sp.*

7 *Canna sp.*

8 *Verbena bonariensis*

9 *Lepechinia salviae*

10 *Acer palmatum cultivars*

Miscanthus sinensis
'Ghana'

I've experimented with lots of miscanthus over the years. Tall, broad-leaved *M. sacchariflorus* is the perfect seasonal hedge plant while *M. gracilis*, with its fine fountain form, makes for dramatic border punctuation, but for autumn colour, *M. sinensis* 'Ghana' is the one. Like most miscanthus it is present in the garden year-round, apart from six weeks in spring following its annual cut-back. Flower plumes appear in mid–late summer, lending another layer of interest that lasts beyond the onset of autumn colours. Grow it on a moisture-retentive but free-draining soil in blazing sun to get the best autumn leaf tones of orange-red and russets. *Panicum virgatum* 'Squaw' is a shorter alternative grass with flaming autumn leaves.

H/S 1.8m × 1m
Season of colour: Fls: midsummer–spring; Fol: virtually year-round
Colour combination: purple/violet/grey-blue/white/dark purple-brown
Grow it with: *Hosta sieboldiana*
Follow-on plant: *Fritillaria imperialis* (to accompany emerging miscanthus foliage)

Crocus speciosus

Crocuses are not just the harbingers of spring, many of the clan, such as *C. speciosus* and *C. sativa* (saffron crocus) emerge at the other end of the year to grab the last rays of autumn sun. Flowers appear long before the leaves, stretching out of the earth to produce elegant goblets in a pale violet-blue with darker venation. Though they can be naturalised in grass, the flowers last longer in a more protected spot away from blasting winds and battering rain. A free-draining soil is essential, too. Grow them in full sun to lightly dappled shade on a gritty, open soil. They look magical among the fading ferns in the nuttery at Sissinghurst Castle, in Kent.

H/S 15–20cm × 6cm
Season of colour: Fls: late autumn; Fol: winter–spring
Colour combination: light pink/orange/light green/purple/yellow
Grow it with: *Lavandula angusitfolia* 'Hidcote'
Follow-on plant: *Crocus tommasinianus*

LATE AUTUMN

Sternbergia lutea

Unlike the autumn crocuses and their allies this plant bears its dark green, strappy leaves, just before its strong yellow flowers appear. This gives it a real weight and presence at the border front, particularly against the backdrop of burnished autumn foliage. I've seen it at its most beautiful with the red leaves of *Euonymus alatus* sprinkled through its blades and blooms. It will flower for 3–4 weeks, so long as you protect against molluscs. Grow it in sun on a free-draining soil, planting new bulbs in late summer. Split and divide, when required, in spring.

H/S 15–20cm × 6cm
Season of colour: Fls: late autumn; Fol: winter–spring
Colour combination: red/orange/orange-brown/violet
Grow it with: *Euonymus alatus*
Follow-on plant: *Crocus tommasinianus*

Malus × robusta **'Red Sentinel'**

Late autumn sees this small upright tree bejewelled with rich-red spherical fruits which hang like cherry raindrops on the fine grey-brown stems till midwinter and beyond. It starts the year with typical applish blossoms of white and pink which are loved by bees and can serve as a pollinator for nearby apples. Fruits follow in summer but don't take on their glossy cherry look till autumn. If you can steel yourself to remove a few from the display they make good crab apple jelly. Plant the tree in full sun. It will tolerate most soils, but does best on rich but fairly free-draining sites. Use a short stake on the side of the tree that faces the prevailing wind.

H/S 6m × 5m
Season of colour: Fls: spring; Fol: spring–autumn
Colour combination: white/dark green/orange/purple
Grow it with: *Clematis cirrhosa* 'Wisley Cream'
Follow-on plant: *Narcissus poeticus* var. *recurvus*

Saxifraga
'Wada'

Among the bold colours of autumn the understated flowers of this oriental saxifraga add light relief with a dusting of white stars. These delicate blooms call for closer inspection, revealing uneven upper and lower petals which virtually float above the plant. It feels very much like a heuchera in form but with more exciting flowers and slightly more challenging growing requirements. It will survive in full shade but I've found it happiest in dappled shade, where beams of light pick out its late flowers. Soil should be woodsy and moisture-retentive but sandy enough to stop it rotting off over winter. S. 'Black Ruby' has deep purple foliage and dark pink flowers and is an equally worthy cultivar.

H/S 40cm × 40cm
Season of colour: Fls: autumn; Fol: virtually year-round (semi-evergreen)
Colour combination: violet/red/purple/orange-brown/white
Grow it with: *Crocus speciosus*
Follow-on plant: *Galanthus elwesii* var. *monostictus*

Calluna vulgaris
'Wickwar Flame'

The light purple-pink flowers and gold foliage of this heather can go unnoticed in summer, but come autumn it turns chameleon, transitioning from gold to burnished shades of copper and orange which remain striking through to spring. Silver or buff foliage serves as a useful backdrop or it works in a container where it can sidle up to autumn blues such as *Aster* 'Little Carlow'. Its downside? It will only tolerate acid soils, so requires an altered soil or pot culture in an ericaceous compost. *Erica gracilis*, from South Africa, is another useful heather. It's not hardy, but its large, dark pink-red flowers are irresistible for growing in pots for temporary autumn effect.

H/S 30cm × 40cm
Season of colour: Fls: summer–autumn; Fol: year-round
Colour combination: red/orange/violet/blue
Grow it with: *Artemisia schmidtiana* 'Nana'
Follow-on plant: *Iris* 'George'

Salvia longistyla

It takes this sage every day of summer and much of autumn to reach its flowering height of around 2.5 metres, but it's worth the wait. Tuck this beast of a alvia at the back of a border, with rich soil in full sun where its well-textured foliage can provide backdrop to a series of earlier flowerers. Then, through mid- and late autumn, set against blue skies and golden rays, it glows with a mass of skinny, tubular true-red flowers. It can hold its own without staking but sometimes requires reigning in to stop it shading out other plants. Great paired with bold cannas and dahlias.

H/S 2.5m × 1m
Season of colour: Fls: autumn; Fol: spring–autumn
Colour combination: orange/violet/blue/purple/green
Grow it with: *Canna* 'Musifolia'
Follow-on plant: *Allium hollandicum* 'Purple Sensation'

Fothergilla major

For me, nothing tops this shrub for autumn colour foliage. Sure, it's not thrilling for the rest of the year, with its little white bottlebrush flowers in spring and mid-green crinkly foliage, but for three weeks in autumn it will stop you in your tracks. It is often described as a 2-metre and more shrub, but I've rarely seen it get taller than 1.5 metres, making it ideal mid-border or as a woodland edger. It will happily grow in dappled shade but full sun will guarantee a bevy of autumn hues from orange and yellow through to purple and red. Unfortunately, it needs an acid soil to thrive but can be kept happy on a neutral one with a little acidification.

H/S 1.5m × 1.2m
Season of colour: Fls: spring; Fol: spring–autumn (great autumn colour)
Colour combination: violet/blue/purple/green
Grow it with: *Camellia* × *vernalis* 'Yuletide' (as acid-loving backdrop)
Follow-on plant: *Camellia* × *vernalis* 'Yuletide' (flowers once the *Fothergilla's* leaves have fallen)

Fuchsia magellanica

Come late autumn, after six months of flowering, this tough hardy fuchsia is still going strong. Its violet-blue and purple flowers sit well with rich autumn tones, but for those seeking more subtle colours, some of its equally long-flowering relatives are worth a grow. The very pale pink *F.* var. *molinae* and white *F.* 'Hawkshead' have similar flowering seasons and provide a pale contrast to autumn's richer hues. All these shrubs can become wiry and malformed over time, but with a hard prune to 15cm from the ground every few years, they maintain a balanced bun form with an even distribution of blooms. Grow in full sun to partial shade on most soils.

H/S 2m × 2m
Season of colour: Fls: summer–late autumn; Fol: spring–autumn
Colour combination: violet/purple/green/white/dark pink
Grow it with: *Hydrangea macrophylla* 'Hot Red Violet'
Follow-on plant: *Tulipa* 'Burgundy'

Mahonia nitens 'Cabaret'

Mahonias are often consigned
to supermarket car park
planting strips, but this new
cultivar is a sure-fire garden
plant. It sees in late summer
with spiked racemes of
orange-red buds, which
eventually pop to reveal light
yellow-orange flowers which last
well into winter. These pique the
interest of late pollinators and
eventually become attractive,
bluish, grape-like fruits. Its other
USP is a compact habit – it
forms a 1-metre ball over
several years. As it's a new plant,
I've yet to observe its long-term
performance but it has shone
through its first winter. Tolerant
of most soils, it will bloom
best in full sun. Pruning is
not required.

H/S 1m × 1m
Season of colour: Fls: winter;
Fol: year-round
Colour combination: red/
orange-brown/violet/light green/
yellow-green
Grow it with: *Miscanthus*
'Ghana'
Follow-on plant: *Tulipa*
'Red Power'

Callicarpa bodinieri var. giraldii 'Profusion'

With a long-lasting berry colour, quite unlike any other, this
deciduous shrub earns its place in the autumn garden. As its leaves
fade to yellow so the violet berries become evident, finally coming
to prominence in late autumn once the foliage has dropped. Borne
in clusters, the berries need good light and a backdrop of silver
foliage or contrasting orange leaves to truly shine. It reaches some 3
metres when mature and is best grown in multiples, to ensure
pollination and berry profusion. A spot in full sun close to a path
edge allows you to get up close and personal with the berries. It
tolerates most soils.

H/S 3m × 2m
Season of colour: Fls: summer; Fol: spring–autumn
Colour combination: yellow/orange/orange-brown/red/
light green/grey
Grow it with: *Thuja occidentalis* 'Rheingold'
Follow-on plant: *Luzula sylvatica* 'Aurea'

10 MORE LATE AUTUMN PLANTS

1. *Nemesia denticulata* 'Confetti'
2. *Rosa* Flower Carpet White
3. *Rosa* 'Ballerina'
4. *Rosa × odorata* 'Bengal Crimson'
5. *Hydrangea macrophylla* 'Ayesha'
6. *Fuchsia × bacillaris*
7. *Amaryllis belladonna*
8. *Aster* 'White Climax'
9. *Salvia leucantha*
10. *Chrysanthemum sp.*

POTS OF
COLOUR

POTS *of* COLOUR

Well-stocked pots are essentially portable mini gardens. By placing them near the house or by seating we can get up-close to an array of colourful plants.

Larger pots, used as focal points, can lead you around the garden, through entrances and even stop you in your tracks. But perhaps the most useful aspect is that they allow the creation of growing environments that don't otherwise exist in the garden. Acid-loving plants such as camellias won't tolerate most neutral or alkaline soils but thrive in pots of ericaceous compost. Alpines that call for super-sharp drainage and would suffer in heavy-soiled gardens flourish in containers filled with the right gritting mix. Even aquatic plants can be grown in watertight containers.

Pot growing also allows the luxury of being able to ship plants into the limelight when they peak and out of the way as they fade. And of displaying short-term disposable plants such as pot chrysanthemums in autumn and bedding plants in summer. This is a dynamic way to grow, but a total refresh each season arguably provides even more colour. That said, it's perfectly possible to create a permanent 365-planting in a single pot. A simple trio of the right plants such as Viburnum tinus (in lollipop form), early and late tulips and Salvia x jamensis will see a single 80-litre pot in flower year-round.

Because plants in pots are elevated, access and maintenance is easier. Being able to get at them from all angles means you can pack in more plants than you'd ever dream of doing in a border. This is because it's easy to tweak, stake and trim plants to stop them from swamping one another.

Beyond all the cultural and maintenance advantages of growing in pots, I find them ideal for trialling colour ideas and plant association before I commit to a full planting scheme in the garden. They're perfect little dioramas for experimenting with colour which has led to many a daring combo making the transition from pot to plot in the gardens I've looked after.

CONTAINER-GROWING BASICS

✷ Always choose 'frostproof' pots. It's not an absolute guarantee that they will endure every winter, but they'll withstand bitter nights better than their cheaper alternatives, which is ultimately less expensive.

✷ Use pot feet to prevent winter waterlogging and allow air circulation.

✷ Line pots with bubble wrap which is malleable enough to flex when water in the compost freezes in winter.

✷ Avoid using pots with a small neck and wider base. Once plants are well rooted through they are very difficult to get out.

✷ It's all down to personal taste but I tend to go for as plain a pot as possible so the plants do the talking.

✷ A mix of shapes always works well but I usually pick the same-coloured pots when placing them in a cluster. This unifies the group and prevents the pots themselves becoming the visual pull.

✷ The cheapest of fold-up sack barrows makes staging containers and moving them a lesser risk to both the pots and our backs.

✷ Drainage material in the bottom of the pot is vital for long-term plantings. Broken crocks work well but only if they are placed like a series of humpbacked bridges on top of one another. Laid flat they serve little purpose and can actually hinder drainage. Broken polystyrene packaging also works well and makes the pot lighter.

✷ Always use a slow-release feed in the substrate. Most basic composts have little more than six weeks' feed in them, meaning you'll have months of hand-feeding to contend with otherwise.

✷ Small pots can be cute but spell trouble on the watering front, especially at the height of summer.

✷ Saucers beneath pots can make watering more efficient, but be aware that it can lead to plants becoming waterlogged and their compost anaerobic.

✷ Avoid surface rooting problems in your plants by carrying out regular heavy waterings that saturate all the compost in the pot rather than just the first few centimetres or so.

✷ Get to know your pots and containers and also the plants they contain so that you can make informed decisions about when to water.

✷ Don't trust the relative wetness or dryness of the first few centimetres of compost as an indication of overall moisture. Pots often dry from the bottom first.

CREATING VIBRANT POTS

Three Summer-long container recipes

Bedding plants, which are usually highly bred annual species from warm climes, often have very long flowering seasons. This makes them ideal for creating extended summer colour displays in pots. These three recipes are easy to create and maintain.

● **A** *Pelargonium* 'Surcouf', **B** *Dichondra argentea* 'Silver Falls', **C** *Salvia officinalis* 'Purpurascens', **D** *Plectranthus argentatus* 'Silver Shield', **E** *Calibrachoa* Cabaret Purple Glow, **F** *Salvia* 'Wendy's Wish' (below)

● *Fuchsia boliviana, Pennisetum glaucum* 'Purple Majesty', *Verbena* Trailing Lanai™ Royal Purple, *Elymus magellanicus, Petunia* Crazytunia Red Blues

● *Scaevola aemula* New Wonder, *Solanum rantonnetii, Sanvitalia* 'Golden Aztec', *Zinnia* 'Profusion Orange'

Year-round container colour

Creating pots that carry colour through every season makes for an engaging challenge, but by relying on certain key species, which are renowned for their longevity (see page 116 onwards), it's very doable. Choose a pot of 80 litres or bigger and a loam-based compost with coir added to keep the mix open. Fill the bottom of the pot with crocks or polystyrene and layer the inside (not the bottom) with bubble wrap. Add the compost and some slow-release fertiliser ready for planting. Any of the three recipes below will give you year-round colour in the form of flowers and foliage.

Three year-long container recipes

● *Astelia chathamica* 'Silver Spear', *Erysimum* 'Bowles's Mauve', *Nemesia denticulata* 'Confetti', *Tulipa* 'Apricot Parrot', *Muscari comosum* 'Plumosum'

● *Cordyline* 'Cherry Sensation', *Geranium* Rozanne, *Salvia* x *jamensis* 'Hot Lips', *Narcissus* 'Tête-á-Tête', *Muscari comosum* 'Plumosum'

● *Clematis* Fleuri, *Hebe* 'Heartbreaker', *Erigeron karvinskianus*, *Muscari comosum* 'Plumosum'

Bidens, Nemesia and Verbena make for a striking combination as their colours sit opposite on the colour wheel.

Four months of spring colour by layering bulbs

By planting bulbs in layers on top of one another (depending on their needs) it's possible to have a long-running spring display in the smallest of spaces. Bulbs are surprisingly tolerant of this treatment and some combinations can keep performing over several years.

STEP I

Prepare the pot

Ready the pot for planting by layering broken crocks and gravel at the bottom and placing a single layer of bubble wrap around the inside of the container (not on the bottom). Ensure the drainage hole is kept open by placing a curved crock over the top of it. Site the pot in its final position before filling with compost to save having to moving it later.

STEP 2

Compost and feed

Many bulbs, such as tulips, produce feeding roots shortly after planting in late autumn. Given that their flowering is some 4–5 months off, they require enough feed to see them through till spring. Mix a slow-release six-month granule into a 50/50 mix of general-purpose peat-free compost and John Innes 3.

STEP 3

First and second layer of bulbs

Choose late-flowering tall-stemmed tulips to form the deepest layer of bulbs some 20cm below the finished soil level. Cover them with the compost, ensuring they're topped with around 5cm of mix. Position the next layer of bulbs – this could be mid-season narcissus or tulips. Add another layer of soil on top of the bulbs.

STEP 4

Next layer of compost in

Around 5cm below the finished soil level, place the crocus bulbs randomly across the compost surface. Complete the planting by bringing the compost level up to within a few centimetres of the top of the pot. Firm the compost using fingertips rather than patting the top surface, which does little to settle the compost around the bulbs.

STEP 5

Water and mulch

Water in the bulbs. This has the dual function of settling the bulbs in and letting them know (along with the cold weather) that it is time to start growing. Mulch the top of the pot to prevent compost splashing out. Keep the substrate moist but not sodden until after the flowers appear in Spring.

Less is more in this simple understated combination. The grouping of *Euphorbia* 'Diamond Frost', *Nemesia* and *Chlorophytum* will ensure colour from early summer till late autumn.

Left Creating vibrant and dynamic container plantings relies on grouping plants which complement and contrast with one another in foliage, colour and form. Container growing also affords the opportunity to cram in plants which would struggle to grow in such close proximity in a border. A pot planting allows us to get up close and personal with the plants, clipping, staking and finessing them to avoid one species dominating the others. This combination of Petunia, Nemesia, Salvia and Cleome at East Ruston Old Vicarage in Norfolk will ensure the container carries colour from early summer till the first frosts (7 months).

Top Foliage colour is as important as flowers in this clever combination. The flecks and spikes of gold and pale blue leaves are the perfect counter point to the rich red and blue blooms. This pairing preventa the pot becoming too heavy in either colour or texture. 6-7 months colour.

Bottom left Frequent repetition of colour and texture holds this subtle mix of burgundy, peach and silver together outside the walled garden at East Ruston Old Vicarage. Plectranthus argentatus provides the silver foliage while a trailing Verbena delivers burgundy blooms and a bedding Begonia provides the peach petals. It will bloom for up to seven months.

Bottom right This planting plays it safe with an analogous palette of annuals in violets and blues with white for a gentle lift. With good regular feeding the colour will stay fresh across nearly 3 seasons.

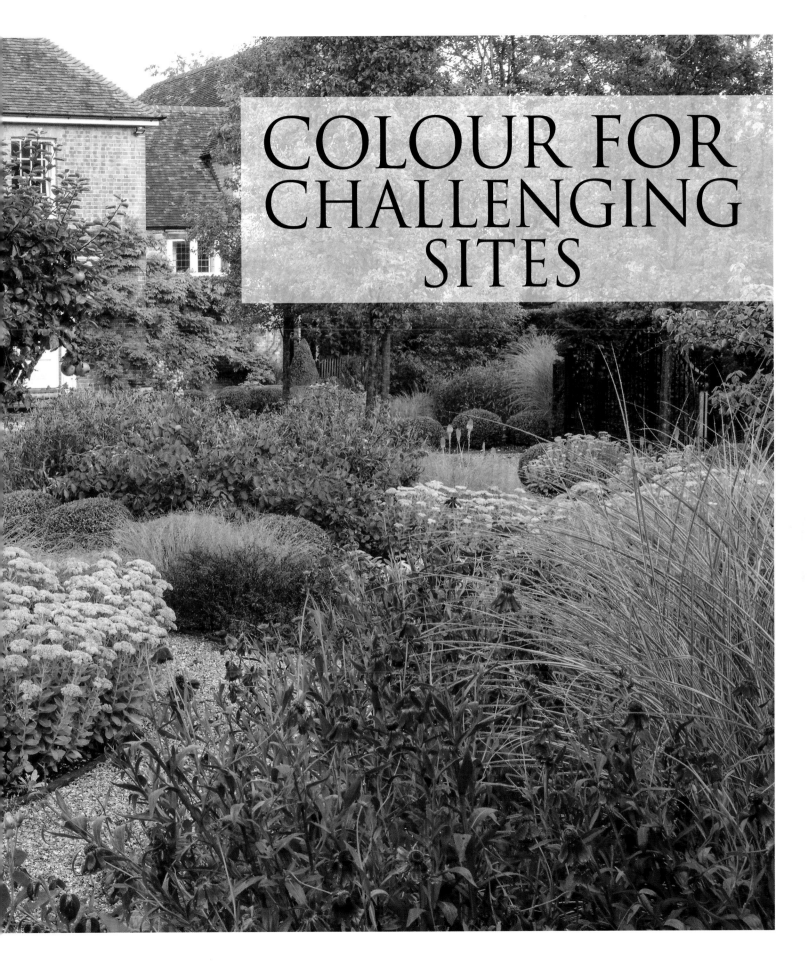

COLOUR FOR CHALLENGING SITES

YEAR-ROUND COLOUR *for* CHALLENGING SITES

We've all got those difficult bits in the garden where microclimate, soils or established plants make growing for year-round colour a particular challenge. Although these troublesome spots can appear onerous to resolve, with the right palette of plants they can become an opportunity to grow a wider range of interesting species.

Dry-shade areas, the bane of most gardeners, will support an array of colour-rich plants capable of delivering the goods 365 days a year. Equally, baked and parched hot spots with free-draining soil will support a host of plants in myriad colours through the seasons. Guidance on choosing plants for these spots and others is best sought from Mother Nature herself. In the wild, dry shade often occurs around the base of thirsty, heavy canopied trees and shrubs. Those plants that have made this environment their home have evolved and adapted to survive on little water and scant light. Some have large leaves to garner energy from even the weakest beam of light, others are deep-rooted and some (especially those under deciduous trees) do all their growing and flowering in winter and early spring while the trees above them are without leaves. In contrast, plants that have evolved to withstand sun-baked, free-draining environments have a different set of adaptations. Some coat their leaves in a silvery powder or fine hairs which act as sunblock, others have complex underground water-storage systems or tiny leaves to reduce water loss.

All these adaptations can work to our advantage as gardeners, meaning that if we choose the right plants (as determined by Mother Nature) they will naturally survive in these difficult environments without us struggling to keep them alive. So, rather than bemoan the difficulties of these challenging environments, I like to see them as opportunities to try out plants I may not have ever considered otherwise.

Geranium x *oxonianum* brings fresh flowers to dry shade areas for months on end.

Bone-dry and shady

Populating lightless, parched areas is relatively easy through winter and spring as soil moisture levels are higher and trees are out of leaf, allowing more light to reach the ground. The greater challenge comes in summer, as the overhead canopies furnish with leaves and all life is doing battle for the available water. *Galium odoratum*, one of the few plants that manages to grow under the dense canopy of beech woodland, is a solid doer in this situation. From late spring and on into summer it sparkles with clusters of bright white, sweetly scented flowers. It can be a bit of a rampant spreader but that trait is more than tolerable in dry shade where it reaches little more than 30cm high. Clumps can be easily split and replanted in spring, before flowering, which usually lasts 3–4 months.

For truly long-flowering species that thrive in dusty shade, I turn to three stalwarts – geranium, fuchsia and tiarella. These grin-and-bear-it plants muster up to six months of flower with scant regard for unpleasant growing conditions. *Geranium* x *oxonianum*, which has spawned numerous cultivars in shades of pale red-pink, seems to relish the challenge of an impoverished shady site. By mid-spring it has formed a mound of typical palmate leaves, shortly followed by flowers held 10–20cm above the foliage. It will continue to flower in bursts through till autumn but often does best with a cut back in midsummer to trigger a fresh flush of flowers and foliage.

Fuchsia 'Riccartonii' is also highly floriferous, producing small red and dark-violet blooms on its 2-metre and taller shrubby frame from early summer till autumn. Like other dry-shade-tolerant fuchsias, such as *F. magellanica* var. *molinae*, it's borderline hardy and may require winter protection in cooler gardens. A perfect partner for these rich blooms are the pale-pink flowers of *Tiarella* 'Morning Star'. This cultivar is especially long flowering, but like all the tiarellas does best when well-watered in its first year to encourage deep rooting and future water independence. It has palmate geranium-looking foliage, sporting attractive purple-brown markings and forms a tight clump similar to heucheras. For less showy but reliable colour the poppy family offers up the yellow-flowered *Stylophorum lasiocarpum* (page 54) and *Chelidonium majus*. The greater celandine may be viewed as a weed by some, and it certainly seeds around, but for cheery yellow flowers during summer, in shade, I can forgive it promiscuous habits.

As summer submits to autumn so a new tranche of plants provide the colour. Short-lived as they are, the flowers of autumn crocus and colchicum are vital here. Their shades of light pink and blue bring a freshness otherwise lacking in autumn. They often do best where their flowers (which emerge before their leaves) are supported both physically and in colour by other short plants such as galium or *Polystichum vulgare*. On a larger scale, *Aster ageratoides* 'Ashvi' is an autumn delight. It is one of the few asters, along with *A. divaricatus*, that can handle dry shade. It stays short (but slowly spreading) at around 1 metre and produces yellow-centred, starry white blooms

Clockwise from top left
Fuchsia 'Riccartonii', *Tiarella* 'Morning Star', *Aster ageratoides* 'Ashvi' and *Polystichum vulgare* are among a limited set of plants tolerant of growing in dry shade.

from midsummer till the frosts. Also bringing vibrancy to autumn is the ruddy marbled foliage of *Epimedium × rubrum*. This squat epimedium stays evergreen through winter, often developing ever-ruddier tones as the weeks progress. It works as a great foil to the dark strappy leaves of *Iris foetidissima*, with its cracked-open pods of orange seeds which sustain through autumn.

Winter in dry shade situations can be surprisingly colour-rich, with flowers and fruit in violets, pinks and orange. Carrying colour from autumn through into winter is *Pyracantha* 'Orange Glow', with its weatherproof orange berries. It is well set off by the evergreen *Rhamnus alaternus* 'Argenteovariegata', with its cream/green leaves. It has always performed superbly for me in dappled shady spots. On a smaller scale, the evergreen foliage of *Ophiopogon japonicus* 'Variegatus' remains fresh come what may with its longitudinal white stripes, and it looks especially striking when paired with *Cyclamen coum* (see page 203). Vincas come into their own here, too. The small variegated-leaved *Vinva minor* 'Ralph Shugert' glows out of the shade with light violet flowers, while *V. m.* 'Atropurpurea' has dark pink-violet blooms that speak more of summer than winter. *V. difformis* (see page 212) is even earlier into bloom, with flower buds popping from mid-winter onwards. And for spring fresh flowers in the dry shady depths of winter, *Crocus tommasinianus* (see page 213) is worth establishing, too.

As spring arrives the race is on for many plants, particularly bulbs such as bluebells and snowdrops, to flower and set seed before the canopy above them fills with leaves. Hellebores are quick off the mark too. The *Helleborus × hybridus* forms are robust and rich with flower colour, but they only just tolerate dry shade. Other species, such as *H. foetidus* and *H. cyclophyllus* often handle it better. Both have fresh light-green flowers which set off any bright colour you care to place next to them.

Trachystemon orientalis is less well-known but very at ease in dry shade. Its flowers are light blue-violet with an exotic complex structure. They emerge in late winter and are followed by huge leaves which can hold their own until summer but will only sustain beyond this point with regular watering. Other species to consider include the flowering currant *Ribes sanguineum*, *Euphorbia amygdaloides* var. *robbiae*, *Brunnera macrophylla* 'Jack Frost', *Dicentra spectabilis*, Eomecon *chionantha* and Pulmonaria sp.

Top Vinca difformis sparkles in dry shade with white to palest blue flowers.

Bottom Rhamnus alaternus 'Argenteovariegata' will take to life in the shadows.

OTHER PLANTS FOR BONE-DRY SHADY AREAS

- *Alchemilla mollis*
- *Arctostaphylos uva-ursi*
- *Anemanthele lessoniana*
- *Melissa officinalis*
- *Aster divaricatus*
- *Sarcococca sp.*
- *Asarum europaeum*
- *Pachysandra axillaris* 'Crûg's Cover'
- *Viola labradorica*
- *Bergenia* 'Bressingham Ruby'
- *Convallaria majalis*
- *Muscari sp.*
- *Skimmia × confusa* 'Kew Green'
- *Ruscus aculeatus*

" *As spring arrives the race is on for many plants to flower and set seed before the canopy above them fills with leaves.* "

Hot, dry and free-draining

Hot, dry microclimates tend to occur, unsurprisingly, on free-draining soils, but this can be cranked up several notches if other factors are involved. Wind can cause significant desiccation, as can enclosed heat-retaining courtyards, suntraps and south-facing sites. To grow in these harsh environments, or to reduce water use in the garden, requires drought-tolerant plants from Mexico, Turkey, California and beyond. Species from these regions flower across many seasons, meaning it's possible to compile a palette of sun-lovers with floral colour virtually year-round.

Spring's first flurry of flowers in the arid garden is thanks to various bulbs, short perennials and sub-shrubs. Among these, and wonderfully reliable for early colour, are the brassica relatives. *Iberis sempervirens*, better known as candytuft, produces delicate white blooms from its low evergreen frame in spring and continues flowering until summer. *Aurinia saxatilis* 'Citrina' is equally eager to bloom, with its clusters of little pale yellow flowers set off a treat by the silvery mound of foliage from which they protrude. Both are well partnered with any of the numerous purple- or violet-flowered forms of *Aubrietia* and all will flower till the end of spring.

Bulbs work beautifully woven through these early brassicas. *Allium unifolium* appears in mid-spring with short-stemmed flowers in a delicate shade of light pink and continue till early summer. The much-revered *Tulipa sprengeri* is very much at home in the heat, too. It produces vibrant red flowers on 40cm stems in late spring and will (very slowly) bulk up and colonise an area over time. *Ipheion uniflorum*, with its luminous, light blue, starry flowers is speedier and will *freely* colonise dry gravelly areas. More structural plants, such as *Euphorbia characias* subsp. *wulfenii*, are dry garden stalwarts, but for a challenge *Echium wildpretii*, with its spiralling spike of dusky red flowers, is worth a try. Grown from seed it will flower in its second or third year, so long as it's located in very free-draining soil and its rosettes are kept rain-free and not too frosty under a cloche over winter. Spectacular.

As spring rolls into summer so the palette of plants to choose from increases. Notable among the array of silver-leaved shrubs suitable to these sites is *Zauschneria californica*. Unlike so many of its silver-leaved brethren, such as brachyglottis, santolina or phlomis, which have strong yellow flowers, this little chap is resplendent with red blooms.

From top left clockwise
Echium wildpretii,
Zauschneria californica,
***Eremurus* 'Cleopatra'**
and *Lotus hirsutus* all
lap up the heat in
garden hot-spots.

It comes from California where it enjoys sun, sharp drainage and the occasional A-lister wandering past. Equally dramatic is *Iris domestica*. Its humdrum name goes no way to describe its 80cm willowy stems, topped with dramatic orange flowers smattered with red dots. Another orange flower, albeit in a more subtle apricot hue, is *Eremurus x isabellinus* 'Cleopatra'. Known as the foxtail lily, it hails from stony mountainous territory in central Asia. Many gardeners struggle to grow it, but in an arid free-draining garden away from the shadows of other plants it will develop 1.2-metre spikes of flower for around a month in early summer. These tricky plants stand the best chance of establishing when planted on top of a layer of gravel in their planting pit – protected from winter wet.

Easier and more subtle colour comes in the form of *Lotus hirsutus*. This little billowing cloud of a plant has delicate silver foliage and a long succession of white, clover-like flowers. It looks particularly at home in gravel or tumbling over rocks. Many of these summer-flowering sun-lovers produce a couple of months of flower but *Erodium chrysanthum* (see page 124), the geranium relative, outdoes them all, with up to six months of buttermilk-coloured blooms. It positively relishes the heat and gently seeds around, especially in gravel. The choice of plants suited to hot dry spots could fill a book on its own, but *Cerastium*, known as 'snow in summer' due to its silver leaves, white flowers and trailing nature, can't go without a mention. Equally, the lovely pale blue rock bindweed *Convolvulus sabatius* is a must-have, but for real summer wow, the crook-necked flower stems and perfoliate young-eucalyptus-like foliage of

Above left to right
Convolvulus sabatius,
Sedum 'Purple Emperor'
and *Iris unguicularis* 'Mary
Barnard' bring colour to
summer, autumn and
winter respectively.

Parahebe perfoliata are sublime. A true choice plant, this diminutive Antipodean lovely carries pale-blue flowers over several months and will re-bloom in autumn with a cut back.

Also carrying flowers into autumn are cultivars of *Sedum telephium*. This drought-tolerant plant thrives in the heat with cultivars such as *S. t.* 'Purple Emperor' getting ever more tanned with the sun's rays. Another great summer-to-autumn carry-over plant is the ubiquitous *Verbena bonariensis*. Its tall stems dotted with clusters of pink-violet flowers keep going till the frosts and readily self-seed (ready for next year) into dry soils and gravel. Its cousin, the short mound-forming *V.* 'La France', has light violet flowers and will overwinter in dry soil on a protected site.

Fresh into flower for autumn is the unusual *Serratula seoanei*. It is short, at 30cm, and has many aster qualities. Light pink-violet flowers sustain through much of autumn and its frail 30cm exoskeleton lasts throughout winter. Once the truly cold weather hits the arid garden in early winter, foliage stalwarts such as *Yucca gloriosa* 'Variegata', silver *Onopordum*, and any of the rosette-forming *Eryngiums* carry the colour, but come late winter the flowers begin again. Reticulata iris, in all their tones from palest blue to deepest violet, love the free-draining soil of the arid garden and will deliver an early burst of colour for three weeks or so. Longer lasting is *Iris unguicularis* 'Mary Barnard', but best of all and carrying colour for 5–6 weeks is *Scilla* 'Tubergeniana'. Forming spikes of pale-blue flower, as opposed to the more common scillas which bloom on short stems, it holds its own till the creeping brassicas begin again in early spring.

OTHER PLANTS FOR HOT, DRY AND FREE-DRAINING SITES

- *Helianthemum sp.*
- *Ornithogalum pyrenaicum*
- *Bupleurum falcatum*
- *Osteospermum sp.*
- *Gaura sp.*
- *Gladiolus papilio*
- *Cistus sp.*
- *Convolvulus cneorum*
- *Crinum × powellii*
- *Glaucium flavum*
- *Lavandula sp.*
- *Phlox douglasii*
- *Asphodeline lutea*
- *Linaria purpurea*
- *Scilla peruviana*
- *Sedum sp.* (dwarf forms)
- *Sempervivum sp.*
- *Agapanthus sp.*
- *Anaphalis sp.*
- *Ballota sp.*
- *Cichorium intybus*
- *Dierama sp.*
- *Foeniculum vulgare × Halimiocistus*
- *Iris sp.* (bearded forms)

Shady walls

Walls that wallow in the shadows replicate some aspects of woodland environments, so climbers that naturally reside under the canopy really work here. Plants from the woodlands of China, Japan, Myanmar and the US are well adapted to shade, rain shadows and the other unpleasant conditions that a north wall presents. Growing several of them together creates a richer tapestry of colour and texture, but the trick is to combine plants that form peaceful coalitions without smothering one another. As pairs or trios these plants can keep the colour up year-round, so long as they are well supported, guided and trained. Timber trellis can be useful for this, and looks good for a few years, but all too often it gets pulled away from the wall due to stems thickening behind it or the sheer weight of the plant. The most versatile and long-lasting option I've found is to screw in vine eyes and straining wire. Installed at 30cm intervals horizontally across the wall; this system suits many climbers and the wire can be tightened or easily replaced when required.

A select few cultivars among garden classics such as roses and clematis will grow on shady walls. Of the roses, *Rosa* 'Danse du Feu', with its repeating red flowers, always does well. It can be combined with clematis such as *Clematis* 'Henryi', with its large white flowers, vigorous habit and long season. Pairings such as this work well but only cover the summer season. For a longer run of colour the more unusual *Schisandra rubriflora* works a treat. In late spring it produces small, exotic-looking red flowers that by midsummer have become delicate chains of creamy-white seeds (right). As summer progresses the seeds become red and hold on well into autumn. To ensure good pollination, and therefore berries, male and female plants need to be grown side by side. In contrast, *Parthenocissus quinquefolia*, the Virginia creeper, is happy on its own. It quickly colonises shady vertical planes, clinging on to virtually anything with its tendril-mounted gripping discs. Its leaves are reliably lush from spring till autumn when they take on stunning shades of red, enhanced by warm days and cool nights.

To carry colour through winter relies on clematis and ivy species. *Clematis* armandii, from China and Myanmar, has thick, waxy, dark green leaves and an abundance of white flowers in late winter and early spring. It needs the occasional dead chunk cutting out of it but otherwise it is fairly trouble free. *Hedera algeriensis* 'Gloire de Marengo' holds its marbled leaves through winter and doesn't tend to look as sickly as cultivars such as *H. colchica* 'Sulphur Heart', which can appear dried out and miserable through winter. The climbing *Hydrangea anomala* subsp. *petiolaris* and its close cousin *Schizophragma* are also happy on north walls. Both are slow to establish but once their adventitious roots, which appear on the stems, get a grip on the wall they are away. *Schizophragma* possibly trumps the climbing hydrangea with its wide spreading flower heads and white bracts, which look a little like floating feathers, but both are worth a try.

From top left clockwise
Rosa 'Danse du Feu', *Hydrangea anomala* subsp. *petiolaris*, *Clematis* 'Henryi' and *Schizophragma hydrangeoides* can furnish shady walls with colour.

Nigella damascena, Allium christophii (top) and *Clematis tangutica* (bottom) add layers of additional colour to well-established gardens.

Established gardens

An established garden which is lacking flowers in a particular season or has a deathly dull border in July presents a real challenge. Slotting new plants into this sort of garden can mean having to hoick out or hack back existing species to make space – but there is another approach. A special set of plants, which could be labelled as 'plug-in plants', can come to the rescue. These are the sort of plants that don't demand much ground space but do lots up top. The sort of plants that can plug a gap and hold their own, mid-border, in an instant.

One such plant is the heaven-sent and heavily scented *Daphne bhoula* var. *glacialis* 'Gurkha'. The skinny habit of this winter-flowering shrub (H/S 2m × 70cm) means it takes up minimal space at ground level, so it's easy to slot in among existing plants. Its canopy is also open enough not to block light from those surrounding it. It's deciduous and bares numerous pink-budded white flowers in late winter for up to six weeks. This amount of flower from such little space is surely a worthwhile investment. Another skinny plug-in plant is *Miscanthus sinensis* 'Ghana'. This bolt-upright grass forms a neat column of background foliage until autumn and winter, when it comes into its own with leaves in fiery tones of red and orange and flower plumes which last winter-long. Its footprint can be maintained at little more than 60cm wide yet its impact in the border when it reaches 1.8 metres high is huge.

Columnar conifers work well as plug-in-plants, too. *Juniperus scopulorum* 'Skyrocket' has grey-blue foliage and a bean-pole habit (H 5m × S 50cm), meaning it can be parachuted into a bed with minimal impact on existing planting but have maximum colour effect. Best of all for adding lasting colour with a minimal footprint are the

standardised or lollipop shrubs and roses. These can be slotted into a border at their mature size for instant effect. Several evergreens, such as the gold or silver euonymus and red-leaved photinia are grown as standards and provide year-round foliage colour but for old-fashioned exuberance, standard roses are fun. They are usually available as either half-standards (80cm high) or full standards (1m high) – both can be maintained, with the usual pruning, to the same size, year in, year out. *Rosa* 'The Fairy' with its small pink flowers over summer is often available in this form along with the true red *R.* 'Ruby Wedding', and the timeless white *R.* 'Iceberg'. Mature trees and shrubs in an established garden can act as ideal climbing frames for certain twining, tendrilled species which need little ground space but can cloak established plants with flowers and foliage. Yellow-flowered, delicate-leaved *Clematis tangutica* will rampage up established trees reaching six or more metres, providing colour from midsummer to late autumn. *Clematis* × *triternata* 'Rubromarginata' is equally light in foliage but with dark pink and white flowers. It will reach 3–4 metres, making it ideal for growing on shrubs of a similar size.

Roses work well here, too. The brash purple-red *Rosa* 'American Pillar' is an eager rambler that will rampage through larger trees. For more subtle colour, the 6-metre-high white-flowered rambler *R. longicuspis* also works well. Annual climbers are even more useful for adding extra colour. Many of them flower in mid- and late summer and, as such, work perfectly to add another season of interest to spring-flowering shrubs. *Ipomoea* 'Scarlet Rambler', initially grown up a cane, will coat a 2m × 1m shrub in boisterous stems and red flowers in a matter of weeks. The orange-flowered *Eccremocarpus scaber*, usually grown as an

Rosa 'American Pillar' can provide colour to the loftier reaches of the garden as it quickly rampages through trees or over structures.

annual but truly a perennial, can be grown in the same way. It's a little more challenging from seed, but worth the effort.

Bulbs and self-seeders are also an easy addition to established gardens. Tulips and alliums can be planted twixt herbaceous perennials in autumn and with a mix of cultivars can add another two or three months of colour in late spring among the existing planting. *Allium* 'Purple Sensation' is rugged and up to this task, or for really dramatic colour bright yellow *Tulipa* 'West Point' enlivens even the darkest spots. Equally, *Nectaroscordum siculum*, with its multi-tonal pendulous blooms and fairy castle seed heads, can be treated in the same way but brings its colour to the garden in early summer. For midsummer it's worth slotting in *Galtonia candicans*. This bulb produces 1-metre stems carrying giant but elegant, snowdrop-looking white flowers. Other bulbs can be introduced under deciduous shrubs that hold little winter interest. Here, the likes of snowdrops, *Eranthis hyemalis*, and the delightful blue *Anemone blanda* will thrive. Inexpensive self-seeders are worth a shot in the established garden, too. A sneaky extension to the border fronts when they are being cut can give rise to a narrow soil gap that can be populated with nigella, myosotis or escholtzia. Or, it's also worth slotting in pre-grown columnar self-seeders such as digitalis or *Verbena bonariensis*. They'll bloom away in their first year and then go on to colonise even the slightest scrap of soil that suits their tastes in future years.

" Twining, tendrilled species need little ground space but can cloak established shrubs with fresh flowers. "

> *Winter in the wild garden can be punctuated with long-lasting vibrant fruits and hips.*

Viburnum opulus, Rosa 'Fru Dagmar Hastrup', *Rosa* 'Geranium' and *Fragaria vesca* 'White Soul' bring fruitful exuberance to the wild garden.

Wilder areas

Wild or low-maintenance areas of the garden needn't be any less colour-rich through the seasons. Numerous plants, most of which can be left to their own devices after initial establishment, can provide many seasons of colour. An absolute favourite of mine is the wild *Viburnum opulus*. It sees in spring with clusters of white flowers, followed by glossy red berries through late summer and autumn when the foliage takes on rich oranges, reds and yellows. It's so easy to grow it's often used on motorway embankments, but that shouldn't lessen its garden merits. *Euonymus europaeus* 'Red Cascade' has a similar feeling to it, with an open habit and very few demands. It also has several seasons of interest, producing pendulous orange seeds which hang from dark pink cases in late summer and which are eventually accompanied by stunning, burnished, red and bronze foliage in autumn.

Winter in the wild garden can be punctuated with long-lasting vibrant fruits and hips. *Rosa* 'Fru Dagmar Hastrup' is adept at this. Following its sweet, clove-scented pink flowers in summer are pumpkin-shaped hips in red tones through winter. *Rosa*

'Geranium' is even more enchanting, with true-red, single summer flowers and prickly, urn-shaped orange-red hips. Company for these richly-coloured fruits through winter months calls for the ornamental bramble – *Rubus cockburnianus*. Its ghostly white stems glow out of the winter gloom, but it should only be planted where it can truly rampage. It also works well planted with the upright, double pink-flowered *Rubus spectabilis* 'Olympic Double' or one of the tough euphorbias such as *E. ceratocarpa* (see page 119).

These larger shrubs are suited to more substantial gardens, but there are wild things for smaller spaces, too. *Fragaria vesca* 'White Soul', a white alpine strawberry, has it all – pretty white flowers, great weed-suppressing groundcover and a succession of delicious white fruits (which do not interest the birds) from late spring into autumn. Naturalised bulbs work well on the smaller scale, too. The wild *Narcissus pseudonarcissus* can be planted through any of the plants mentioned above along with snowdrops, bluebells and *Eranthis*, all of which will seed around and colonise wild areas.

WINTER
PLANTS

EARLY WINTER

Brassica oleracea

Planting cabbages for colour may seem like a last resort but they have much to recommend them. Ornamental brassicas are totally weather-proof, hold their colour and are easy to maintain. I've used them in containers with so called 'winter bedding' such as pot cyclamen and pansies. These tend to come and go depending on the degree of cold and wet but the cabbages hold fast. Pigeons and slugs occasionally take a fancy to them but they are generally trouble-free, save removing the lower leaves which slowly shed and can cause a terrible stink. They are happy to grow in just about any soil in full sun. Perfect for containers.

H/S 50cm × 30cm
Season of colour: Fls: n/a; Fol: autumn–summer
Colour combination: red/purple/blue/green/orange/violet/white/pink
Grow it with: *Phormium* 'Rainbow Sunshine'
Follow-on plant: *Anemone blanda*

Skimmia japonica subsp. *Reevesiana*

Winter calls for reliability and resistance in plants and this skimmia has it in droves. Through frost and snow it holds it soya-bean-sized, true-red berries in perfect attention-seeking clusters, so much so that you could mistake them for artificial. Skimmias are prone to becoming chlorotic (yellow leaved and wan) if allowed to dry out or get too much sun in summer so I have always used this evergreen shrub as a container plant. Growing it this way means it can be brought to the sun in winter, when it's at its berry-best and returned to dappled shade in summer. *Skimmia japonica* 'Rubella' is worth growing, too. Its tight buds are berry-like over winter but bust into bloom come spring.

H/S 1m × 80cm
Season of colour: Berries: autumn–spring; Fol: year-round
Colour combination: white/light green/violet/purple/orange
Grow it with: *Erica* × *darleyensis* f. *albiflora* 'White Perfection'
Follow-on plant: n/a: best in pot and moved out of site after winter

Clematis urophylla 'Winter Beauty'

Amid the berries and leaves of the winter garden this refined clematis dares to bare its blooms. Borne in clusters, the thick-petaled upturned-urn flowers age from cream to white among its glossy evergreen foliage. Its character is similar to *C. armandii* but without the rampancy and random dead patches. Try it alongside, or even on established winter berry shrubs such as pyracantha and cotoneaster whose fruits-laden stems are freshened with the white blooms. It's not as hardy as some winter clematis so requires a warm sheltered spot – perhaps against the house. Drainage is important, too. Plant it in a woodsy mix but with added grit for sharp drainage. It's a group 1 clematis meaning pruning is simply tidying up wayward stems, if necessary, after flowering in spring.

H/S 2m × 2m
Season of colour: Fls: autumn–spring; Fol: year-round
Colour combination: blue-grey/orange/red/purple
Grow it with/Follow-on plant: *Pyracantha coccinea* 'Red Column'

Beta vulgaris

Why consign a beautiful edible plant to the veg plot when it can provide colour and food in the garden? Bright chards rival just about everything through winter for pure colour punch – especially if they are lit from behind. Glowing ruby red and dark orange-yellow stems topped with dark glossy crinkly leaves bring such vibrancy that I've even used them as punctuation through winter pansies, which often have a 'rest' just when you need their colour the most. Sow in small plugs in mid-spring, planting out into just about any soil in full sun come late spring – they'll remain colour rich throughout winter.

H/S 70cm × 40cm
Season of colour: summer–spring; Fol: summer–spring
Colour combination: orange/purple/blue-grey/dark green/white/yellow
Grow it with: *Astelia chathamica*
Follow-on plant: *Tulipa tarda*

Pseudowintera colorata

New Zealand is home to this rarely-grown evergreen shrub. Unlike its tougher antipodean cousins, hebes and phormiums, it can only survive to -5 degrees, meaning it needs protection in colder gardens. This can be in the form of a sheltered wall or a strung together bamboo frame shrouded in fleece. Such efforts are worth it for the multi-tonal leaves with a pale-yellow base colour, trimmed and blotched with red, not to mention the appealing dusty blue-green tone on the back of the foliage. Grow it in part shade on a humus-rich but free-draining soil for cheery colour 365 days a year.

H/S 1m × 1.5m
Season of colour: Fls: spring; Fol: year-round
Colour combination: purple/blue-grey/red/orange/violet
Grow it with: *Heuchera* 'Ginger Peach'
Follow-on plant: *Ajuga reptans* 'Catlin's Giant'

Libertia peregrinans

Come rain, snow or hail, the dark orange-yellow flaming blades of this tough iris relative stand tall and vibrant. It looks most striking paired with the ever-grey leaves of artemisia or ever-blue foliage of *Juniperus squamata* 'Blue Star'. Though it is most useful through winter, spring sees it produce sprays of white flowers followed by orange seeds which can last into winter. It's tolerant of most soils, even very poor ones, but retains its colour best on a woodsy, free-draining site. It spreads underground to form a dense thicket but does not run out of control.

H/S 40cm × 60cm +
Season of colour: Fls: spring; Fol: year-round
Colour combination: blue-grey/violet/red/purple
Grow it with: *Juniperus squamata* 'Blue Star'
Follow-on plant: *Allium caeruleum*

Fascicularia bicolour

Chile is home to some of nature's quirkier plants such as the monkey puzzle tree and the rodent eating puja! It's also home to this impossibly exotic looking bromeliad. Grow it in a sunny sheltered position on a poor, rubbley soil with sharp drainage and it will thrive. Its clusters of light-blue flowers emerge from dramatic rosettes of rich red foliage – a real boon in the depths of winter. Try it on a bank, in a rock garden or tucked away in a hot corner. It's one of those plants that you visit in the garden rather than place in a prominent position as after flowering time it's not much of a looker!

H/S 50cm × 70cm
Season of colour: Fls: autumn–spring; Fol: year-round
Colour combination: white/blue/red/purple/blue-grey/grey
Grow it with: *Zauschneria californica*
Follow-on plant: *Cerastium tomentosum*

Camellia × vernalis 'Yuletide'

I confess to finding spring-flowering camellias a waste of space that rarely provide a display unfettered by rain, sun or frost. Autumn-flowering species, mainly C. sasanqua, are a different story though. They can flower for a month or more from late autumn with smaller flowers that often don't get as damaged because the really nasty weather has yet to kick in. C. 'Yuletide' delivers the rare treat of red flowers in winter. Its parentage is much debated but it certainly has some sasanqua traits. It's an open upright shrub best grown in dappled shade in an acid soil or in ericaceous compost in a pot close to the house. A winter delight.

H/S 4.5m × 3m
Season of colour: Fls: autumn–winter; Fol: year-round
Colour combination: yellow-green/light green/violet/white/purple
Grow it with: *Euphorbia robbiae*
Follow-on plant: *Euphorbia robbiae*

Prunus × subhirtella 'Autumnalis Rosea'

Appearing in sporadic bursts from early winter through till early spring this delicate pale-pink cherry is actually a shrub that's top-grafted onto a clear stem, creating a lollipop tree. Flowers are small compared to some blousier cherries but borne with enough abundance to compensate for it. The 'tree' works well in pairs to frame an entrance or dotted into a mixed planting where its light canopy casts little shade on those surrounding it. Good winter light and a dark evergreen backdrop shows off its flowers, which are a boon to winter pollinators such as hoverflies. Grow it in a free-draining but moisture retentive soil in full sun.

H/S 5m × 3.5cm
Season of colour: Fls: autumn–spring; Fol: spring–autumn
Colour combination: grey/dark pink/purple/pale violet/violet/blue grey
Grow it with: *Chamaecyparis pisifera* 'Boulevard'
Follow-on plant: *Rosa xanthina* 'Canary Bird'

Hypericum × inodorum 'Kolmapuki' (Magical Pumpkin)

This plant is a real pedigree pooch – cute, compact and possibly over-bred but it's one of the joys of late autumn and early winter. Our native *Hypericum androsaemum* is one of its parents with which it shares similar berries and great longevity as a cut flower. Unlike some hypericums it remains compact, so long as it is hard-pruned in spring. Berries are a mid-orange-red which slowly darken in clusters on the end of stocky, well-leafed stems. Its ball-like form makes it perfect for container display but it will thrive equally well in the garden in sun or part shade on virtually any soil. Flowers are a typical strong yellow and borne from midsummer till early autumn.

H/S 50cm × 50cm
Season of colour: Fls: summer–autumn; Fol: virtually year-round
Colour combination: violet/red/purple/yellow-green/blue
Grow it with: *Uncinia rubra*
Follow-on plant: *Narcissus pseudonarcissus*

10
MORE EARLY WINTER PLANTS

1. *Viola × wittrockiana* (winter pansy)

2. *Cyclamen* sp.

3. *Leucothoe* Scarletta 'Zeblid'

4. *Coprosma* Pacific Sunset

5. *Cotoneaster lacteus*

6. *Phyllostachys aureosulcata* f. *aureocaulis*

7. *Pseudopanax lessonii*

8. *Gaultheria mucronata*

9. *Colletia hystrix* 'Rosea'

10. *Choisya ternata* 'Sundance'

Luzula sylvatica 'Aurea'

Try growing this ever-gold woodrush through a loosely planted area or woodland edge – its raggedy yellow tussocks will lead your eyes to dark areas, unseen in summer. It works well on the peripheries of mixed borders too, where it thrives at the base of established deciduous shrubs becoming an even stronger yellow once the shrubs shed their leaves. I'd avoid pairing it with light pink but warm-coloured cornus or heucheras are happy bedfellows. Brown flowers appear in late spring but with this plant it's all about the foliage. It can be grown on most soils in deep or dappled shade.

H/S 40cm × 40cm
Season of colour: Fls: spring–summer; Fol: year-round
Colour combination: violet/orange/yellow-green
Grow it with: *Crocus tommassianum* 'Barrs Purple'
Follow-on plant: *Pulmonaria* spp.

MID·WINTER

Cyclamen coum

The appearance of these guys in the depths of winter seems heroic yet somehow their fragile looking leaves and flowers thrive. At Chelsea Physic Garden in London a disorderly row of them sit under a hornbeam hedge, happy to grow, flower, set seed and die back, all while the hedge above them is out of leaf. An easy alliance. Left without too much disturbance they will seed and spread in most versions of shade. A variance of this plant known as Pewter Group has pale silver-green leaves, great for a dark spot. Flower colours vary from white to mid-pink but it's the darkest of dark pinks that wins my heart every time.

H/S 15cm × 20cm
Season of colour: Fls: spring; Fol: winter–spring
Colour combination: white/dark pink/grey-blue
Grow it with: *Galanthus* spp.
Follow-on plant: *Mirabilis jalapa* (at the base of a hedge or similar)

Iris unguicularis

For ten months of the year this plant is pretty dull, no, let's be honest, very dull. But, for two months it does what no other winter plant dares to do. It produces huge (10cm wide) blooms composed of pale-blue gossamer thin petals that somehow resist freezing temperatures and jet-propelled rain. This North African plant delights viewers in the garden and wins further fans when cut for the house. Displayed in a 'single stem vase' flowers emanate a gentle scent which hints at spring. Grow it at the base of a south-facing wall. Get the planting conditions perfect by making a 50/50 mix of rubble and gravel with your garden soil. It thrives on razor sharp drainage and neglect. Split and divide in spring every 4–5 years.

H/S 30cm × 50cm
Season of colour: Fls: winter–spring; Fol: year-round
Colour combination: yellow-green/pink/red
Grow it with: *Helleborus argutifolius*
Follow-on plant: *Eschscholzia californica* (grown around the iris)

Correa
'Dusky Bells'

Known as the New Zealand fuchsia, this charming shrub, often described as being tender, has lived through many a frost and low sub-zero night where I have grown it. The trick to keep it going is planting it against a sheltered south-facing wall and ensuring that the soil does not turn into a sticky goop in winter. Given these conditions it will flower through the coldest months till spring. Its form is even and relatively dense with flowers scattered across its surface. Pruning is only required to remove dead, diseased and damaged stems. A perfect mid-winter plant.

H/S 1m × 1m
Season of colour: Fls: winter–spring; Fol: year-round
Colour combination: light violet/white/blue
Grow it with: *Buddleja officinalis*
Follow-on plant: *Thunbergia alata* (grown over the shrub)

Helleborus argutifolius

Bolder in form than most hellebores, this silvery-lime leafed evergreen perennial forms a loose mound of prickle-edged leaves. Standing up to even heavy snow, the flowers emerge in mid-winter aloft its 50cm stems. These are borne in clusters with a good proportion looking up to passers by. The pale lime flowers are a favourite with early pollinators and the plants overall paleness make it a good backdrop for brassier colours such as those of the early iris and scilla. Choose a free-draining soil in full sun and cut back last year's leaves in late spring when the inner core of new stems and leaves have emerged.

H/S 50cm × 1m
Season of colour: Fls: winter–spring; Fol: year-round
Colour combination: orange/red/violet/purple
Grow it with: *Libertia peregrinans*
Follow-on plant: *Galtonia candicans* (planted through the hellebores)

Clematis cirrhosa var. *purpurascens*
'Freckles'

Like a hellebore in the sky; this tough, yet delicate looking clematis is best viewed from below. Grow it over an arch or into a tree where you can peer up to it, backed by the perfect blue sky – if you get lucky, or a damp grey one if not. Either way its cream and burgundy blotched (freckled) blooms bring relief from winter's pared down taupes and browns. And its form has a certain delicacy other winter plants can't muster. Plant it a few centimetres deeper than most plants, part burying the stems. This helps to reduce the chance of clematis wilt – a soil-borne fungal disease.

H/S 5m × 2–3m
Season of colour: Fls: winter–spring; Fol: year-round
Colour combination: yellow-green/white/red
Grow it with: *Euphorbia* × *martini*
Follow-on plant: *Rosa* 'Wedding Day'

Acacia dealbata

I first saw this spectacular Australian tree at RHS Wisley, England, as a student. I was struck to see such an abundance of colour in an otherwise muted landscape of tired green and soggy soil. Its inflorescences of yellow pom-pom flowers are set off against the feathered chalky-blue/grey foliage and do seem a little incongruous – like a canary tussling for crumbs amongst the sparrows, but never the less cheering. Ultimately it forms a substantial tree and is not mad about being pruned so I'd replace it every 10 years or so – it burns ok once it's been seasoned. It's happiest in a warmish spot, on free-draining soil with plenty of sunshine.

H/S 10m × 4m
Season of colour: Fls: winter–spring; Fol: year-round
Colour combination: yellow/orange/red/white/orange-brown
Grow it with: *Phormium* 'Apricot Queen'
Follow-on plant: *Clematis tangutica* (grown through the tree)

Grevillea
'Canberra Gem'

Red is the last colour you'd expect to find in the winter garden but this grevillea has it in abundance from late winter to summer. It's part of the Proteaceae family which is spread across southern Africa, Australia and South America where these plants enjoy blazing sunshine and free-draining soils. Given those conditions, this scratchy looking shrub will establish over five years or so evolving from a mound, to a spikey ball, to a freeform shrub. Grow it in a sheltered spot and provide winter protection from the cold and wet where temperatures sit below -5 degrees for protracted periods.

H/S 2.5m × 2.5m
Season of colour: Fls: winter–summer; Fol: year-round
Colour combination: grey-blue/blue/violet/orange/light green/white
Grow it with: *Astelia chathamica* 'Silver Spear'
Follow-on plant: *Tropaeolum speciosum* (grown through it)

Chimonanthus praecox
'Sunburst'

For most of the year this unassuming Chinese shrub fades into the background, but come early spring its highly scented translucent yellow flowers emerge. Beautiful as they are, these understated blooms need some staging and light direction to look their best. Place the plant so it gets low midday light from behind to illuminate the flowers or against a pale wall as a fan trained shrub. Tolerant of most soils, and requiring little more than an annual thin of one third of the oldest stems after flowering, this is a useful winter shrub in larger gardens.

H/S 1.7m × 1.5m
Season of colour: Fls: winter–spring; Fol: spring–autumn
Colour combination: dark purple/red
Grow it with: *Lophomyrtus* 'Red Dragon'
Follow-on plant: *Hosta sieboldiana* var. *elegans*

10
MORE MID-WINTER PLANTS

1. *Crocus sieberi* subsp. *sublimis* 'Tricolor'
2. *Scilla mischtschenkoana* 'Tubergeniana'
3. *Corydalis cheilanthifolia*
4. *Artemisia stelleriana*
5. *Bellis perennis*
6. *Narcissus cantabricus*
7. *Helleborus × sahini* 'Winterbells'
8. *Helleborus foetidus* Wester Flisk Group
9. *Helleborus* 'Pirouette'
10. *Clematis napaulensis*

Iris reticulata

Depending on the season, dwarf irises emerge from hibernation between late winter and early spring, bringing with them some surprisingly bright hues. *Iris* 'Cantab' is a favourite with blue petals the colour of an electrical spark. *I. r.* 'J.S. Dijt' is a dark violet, virtually invisible against wet soil but radiant with a paler back drop of gravel or silver foliage. And finally, *Iris* 'Katharine Hodgkin' with its Wedgwood-blue and custard coloured petals that don't look of this earth. Strength in numbers is the message here, plant in groups of at least ten bulbs on a free-draining soil in a sunny site or in shallow pots.

H/S 15cm × 15cm
Season of colour: Fls: winter–spring; Fol: spring
Colour combination: yellow/yellow-green/silver/red
Grow it with: *Iris danfordiae/Narcissus cantabricus*
Follow-on plant: *Eryngium × oliverianum*

LATE WINTER

Narcissus
'Rijnveld's Early Sensation'

Often in bloom at the same time as the snowdrops, this reliable daff has a strong yellow on the trumpet face of the flower softened by a dusting of green to the rear. It's fairly storm-proof and thrives in uncompromised sunshine but will put up with a bit of light dappled shade. It looks at its best grouped in scattered clusters of 10 or 20 through a lightly planted scheme, where later-emerging herbaceous perennials will envelope its collapsed leaves. As cut-able as any other daff, it lasts well indoors bringing with it the first hues of spring.

H/S 50cm × 10cm
Season of colour: Fls: winter–spring; Fol: spring
Colour combination: orange-brown/violet/yellow-green
Grow it with: *Carex testacea* (in sun)
Follow-on plant: *Begonia grandis* subsp. *evansii* (in part shade)

Hardenbergia violacea

This antipodean twining climber is not as popular as it deserves to be. It's a pea relative, producing blooms which hang grape-like in pendant racemes – like a less boisterous wisteria. Left to its own devices, in a warm free-draining location, it will twine its way up anything that stays still long enough. I've grown it best on a wrought iron pergola but light timber trellis would work just as well. Grow it in its own space or where it can serve to clothe the bare lower stems of a top-heavy climbing rose. *H. comptoniana*, a close cousin, has delicious purple-mauve flowers but will only tolerate the very warmest spots.

H/S 3m × 3m
Season of colour: Fls: winter-spring Fol: year-round
Colour combination: Pink/purple/violet/light orange-red
Grow it with: *Viburnum* × *bodnantense* 'Dawn'
Follow-on plant: *Eccremocarpus scaber*

Loropetalum chinense 'Black Pearl'

Sometimes branded as too-tender-to-try, I've witnessed this striking shrub see off winters in Norfolk and Canterbury, England. That's not to suggest the plant is bone hardy but that it's worth a shot with protection in a sheltered spot. It's related to witch hazels which is clear when you see its skinny ribbon petals up close. In dappled shade and woodsy soil it will flower from late winter to late spring. Its dark purple-brown evergreen leaves are a challenge to pair with other plants but apricot-coloured heucheras and/or crocosmia strike a balance.

H/S 1.2m × 1.2m
Season of colour: Fls: winter–spring; Fol: year-round
Colour combination: silver/white/light pink/light orange-red
Grow it with: *Acaena microphylla* 'Copper Carpet'
Follow-on plant: *Crocosmia* 'Dusky Maiden'

Prunus mume 'Beni-chidori'

Though I usually pursue long-term colour, this apricot is an exception. Japanese people celebrate the fleeting beauty of plum, cherry and apricot blossoms and I can't help but join them. Lasting 2–3 weeks, at best, the dark pink blooms with their compelling false-eyelash stamens seem impossibly delicate among the tree's skinny stems. Sadly, this cultivar does not produce fruit that is usable, but of course many alternative prunus species do. Grown as a free-standing tree in a protected area or fan-trained on a warm wall in most soils, the blossom is worth the 345-day wait!

H/S 2.5m × 2.5m
Season of colour: Fls: late–winter; Fol: spring–autumn
Colour combination: white/light pink/light violet/light blue/light green
Grow it on: a light-coloured wall
Follow-on plant: *Verbena rigida* (around its trunk at the base of a wall)

Coronilla valentina subsp. glauca 'Citrina'

This compact selection of coronilla hails from Spain and Portugal. It's a very useful long-season legume producing clean light-yellow flowers through winter and spring when all else fails. It will also re-bloom later in summer, sometimes stretching to ten months of colour. Grow it in a sheltered spot in full sun on free-draining soil to make the most of its pale, glaucus blue-green foliage. It does not habitually misbehave rather holding itself in a compact bean-bag form which suits plantings in gravel or as a bit of front border structure. Some claim it will perform in shade, too, but I've yet to try.

H/S 80cm × 1m
Season of colour: Fls: winter–spring–summer; Fol: year-round
Colour combination: light blue-violet/blue/orange-red/light green
Grow it with: *Muscari comosum*
Follow-on plant: *Perovskia atriplicifolia*

Edgeworthia chrysantha 'Red Dragon'

This is not the easiest shrub to grow but success is rewarded with flowers of a colour that's unique in winter. Hailing from Asia, it's fibres are used to make high-quality paper and its flowers are appreciated for their spicy clove scent. Don't risk it if your garden is a frosty hollow but if you've got a warm sheltered spot it's worth a try. It can also be grown in a cold glasshouse or conservatory in full sun or dappled shade. Pruning is only required to remove crossing or overcrowded branches. Get the growing medium right with the addition of organic matter and grit to attain the elusive 'moisture-retentive but free-draining' soil.

H/S 1.5m × 1.5m
Season of colour: Fls: winter–spring; Fol: spring–summer–autumn
Colour combination: light blue-violet/purple/light green
Grow it with: *Sarcococca hookeriana*
Follow-on plant: *Omphalodes cappadocica* (around its base)

Vinca difformis

White flowers with the tiniest suggestion of blue might not seem the greatest relief from dull winter tones but this vinca produces cheery-faced blooms in such abundance that it lifts the spirit. Somewhat more controllable than *V. major*, it still produces stoleniferous stems which arch out and root on contact with the soil. Try it in dry dappled shade where other plants fail and it won't become too troublesome. Flowering from mid-winter to late spring its floral tones evolve from white with a hint of blue to a more distinct light blue later on.

H/S 40cm × infinite (if you don't stop it)
Season of colour: Fls: winter–spring; Fol: year-round
Colour combination: light blue-violet/pink/light green/light green-yellow
Grow it with: *Smyrnium perfoliatum*
Follow-on plant: *Geranium oxonianum*

Cardamine quinquefolia

This beautiful lady's smock is one of the first perennials out of the ground in late winter when it sparkles with blinking-eyed purity. It's a ground-covering woodlander so needs a dappled shade spot that stays moist, or at least damp, year-round. Late winter sees it surge with growth, quickly producing masses of five-fingered leaves and four petaled flowers in light blue-violet with a hint of pink. Come midsummer it retreats below ground level and slowly expands its territory. Try running it under deciduous shrubs at the back of the border or dotting it through other early woodlanders such a *Euphorbia amygdaloides* var. *robbiae*.

H/S 30cm × gently spreading
Season of colour:
Fls: winter–spring;
Fol: winter–spring
Colour combination: light green-yellow/dark pink
Grow it with: *Pachyphragma macrophyllum*
Follow-on plant: *Darmera peltata*

Pulmonaria rubra

Once known as lungworts for their reputed healing properties, pulmonarias are reliable late winter perennials with nearly year-round foliage. Cultivars vary from pure white through purple, violet and blue. *P. rubra* has the standard-issue white-blotched leaves and rarer dusty red flowers which go on till early summer. Given a shear-over after flowering they'll bounce back with a fresh crop of weed-supressing leaves within a few weeks. They're happiest in light shade but can be persuaded to reside in the sun so long as they are on moisture-retentive soil. Avoid letting them dry out – white powdery mildew on the leaves is a sure sign the soil is too dry.

H/S 30cm × 30cm
Season of colour: Fls: winter–spring; Fol: year-round
Colour combination: blue/violet/green
Grow it with: *Helleborus cyclophyllus*
Follow-on plant: *Liriope muscari*

Crocus tommasinianus 'Barr's Purple'

Even during the darkest days of winter this crocus shines thanks to its nearly translucent purple petals and turmeric-smeared stamens. The outside of its six petals alternate between pale and dark – a subtlety best appreciated when the flower is back-lit or potted up. It will readily naturalise by seed or bulbils in rough grass and around trees and shrubs. Corms planted in autumn will flower the following year with one or two heads lasting 2–3 weeks. Choose a free-draining site or improve the soil to avoid excess winter wet. The crocuses look enchanting in terracotta pots, too, where they can be shipped in and out of the limelight in season.

H/S 15cm × 10cm
Season of colour: Fls: winter–spring; Fol: spring
Colour combination: yellow/light yellow/dark purple-red/light orange
Grow it with: *Eranthis hyemalis* 'Orange Glow'
Follow-on plant: *Ipheion uniflorum* 'Wisley Blue'

10 MORE LATE-WINTER PLANTS

1. *Hamamelis × intermedia* 'Diane'
2. *Scilla siberica*
3. *Corylopsis pauciflora*
4. *Stachyurus praecox*
5. *Sycopsis sinensis*
6. *Acacia baileyana*
7. *Corylopsis spicata*
8. *Abeliophyllum distichum* Roseum Group
9. *Azara microphylla*
10. *Bergenia cordifolia* 'Purpurea'

GARDENS *to* VISIT *for* INSPIRATION

Inspiration for planting schemes, colour combinations and garden layouts can come from sources broad and various. Some of the best ideas I've seen are tucked away in private gardens that are open but once or twice a year under a charity scheme such as the UK's National Garden Scheme. These gardens, created by and for the enjoyment of their owners, often have quirks and experiments you might not see elsewhere. On a grander scale, I'm always drawn to visit gardens when I'm travelling overseas and have made many pilgrimages to great gardens of repute. The gardens I'm recommending here are renowned for their longevity, planting schemes and colour associations, be they modern or historic. Be sure to check the relevant website for opening information before you plan a visit.

UK

GREAT DIXTER - Northiam, Rye, East Sussex, England
Exceptional plantsman's garden, created by the late, great Christopher Lloyd, with spectacular colour displays. The place for daring colour combos.
www.greatdixter.co.uk

SISSINGHURST CASTLE - Sissinghurst, Cranbrook, Kent, England
World-famous garden of intricate plantings and sensational colour arranged in hedged rooms; best known for its white garden.
www.nationaltrust.org.uk/sissinghurst-castle-garden

EAST RUSTON OLD VICARAGE - East Ruston, nr Stalham, Norfolk, England
A garden of lush, extravagant plantings and beautiful colour. The Dutch and Exotic areas are of particular note.
www.e-ruston-oldvicaragegardens.co.uk

ANGLESEY ABBEY - Lode, nr Cambridge, Cambridgeshire, England
Dramatic winter garden with inspirational colour plantings, plus open parkland and formal areas.
www.nationaltrust.org.uk/anglesey-abbey

RHS CHELSEA FLOWER SHOW – The Royal Hospital, London, England
The world's best garden show with exceptional show gardens featuring experimental and adventurous colour plantings.
www.rhs.org.uk/shows-events/rhs-chelsea-flower-show

HIDCOTE MANOR - Chipping Campden, Gloucestershire, England
Exceptional world-class Arts and Crafts garden with roomed plantings in rich and various colour schemes.
www.nationaltrust.org.uk/hidcote

FRANCE

CHATEAU AND JARDINS DE VILLANDRY – 37510, Villandry, France
These renowned medieval castle gardens are a polychromatic patchwork of colour for most of the year.
www.chateauvillandry.fr/en

FOUNDATION CLAUDE MONET - Giverny, Haute-Normandie, France
Famed garden of the Impressionist painter. Maintained today in the style and colour combinations developed by Monet.
www.fondation-monet.com/en

INTERNATIONAL FESTIVAL OF GARDENS - Chaumont-Sur-Loire Jardins, Loire, France
Numerous annual season-long show gardens push the boundaries of garden design and colour use. Inspirational.
www.domaine-chaumont.fr/en

HOLLAND

KEUKENHOF - Stationsweg 166a, 2161 AM Lisse, Holland
Extraordinary garden dedicated to bulbs. Swathes of colour illuminate the landscape with tulips, unsurprisingly, playing a central role.
www.keukenhof.nl/en

DE HEERENHOF - Veldstraat 12a, 6227 SZ, Maastricht, Holland
A small but beautifully coloured garden with formal topiary interplanted with inspiration colour pairings.
www.gardenvisit.com/garden/de_heerenhof_maastricht

PRIONA GARDENS - Schuinesloot, Holland
Created by the late, great plantsman and gardener Henk Gerritsen, these laid-back gardens are rich with surprising colour combinations.
www.gardenvisit.com/garden/priona_tuinen

GERMANY

HERMANNSHOF (in Weinheim)
A huge perennial plant collection fills this garden with colour through much of the year. Planting is in the new-wave style.
www.gardenvisit.com/garden/sichtungsgarten_hermannshof

WESTPARK - Westendstrasse, Munich, southwest Germany
Public park with extensive perennial planting in the new-wave style, providing long seasons of colour interest.
www.gardenvisit.com/garden/west_park_munich

KARL-FOERSTER-GARTEN - Am Raubfang 6, 14469 Potsdam-Bornim, Germany
Small, beautiful garden of the famed nurseryman and plant breeder. Many seasons of colour in the new-wave planting style.
www.gardenvisit.com/garden/karl-foerster_garten

AUSTRALIA AND NEW ZEALAND

CLOUDEHILL GARDENS - 89 Olinda-Monbulk Road, Olinda, Victoria, Australia
Pristine planting set in an inspirational landscape with many beautiful planting schemes and quirky ideas.
www.cloudehill.com.au

AYRLIES - 125 Potts Road, Howick, Auckland, New Zealand
Sublime planting woven through flowing, sinuous lines of paths and turf make this colour-rich garden an inspiration hotpot of ideas.
www.ayrlies.co.nz

MAPLE GLEN - Wyndham Letterbox Road, Wyndham, New Zealand
Stunning 20-acre, year-round garden with many growing environments, interesting plants and carefully considered colour use.
www.mapleglen.co.nz

USA

RIVER FARM GARDENS - 7931 East Boulevard Drive, Alexandria, Virginia, USA
The HQ of the American Horticultural Society features colour-themed plantings and year-round interest from a wide range of species.
www.ahs.org/about-river-farm

LONGWOOD GARDEN - 1001 Longwood Road, Kennett Square, Pennsylvania, USA
This world-renowned 86-acre garden is packed with carefully composed colour associations, often on the grand scale.
www.longwoodgardens.org

FILOLI GARDEN - Canada Road, Woodside, California, USA
Inspired by European Arts and Crafts gardens, this spectacular patch of San Francisco is intensely planted with striking colour combinations.
www.filoli.org

INDEX

Page numbers in *italics* refer to illustrations

GLOSSARY

AUTUMN/FALL
Outside of the tropics, the autumn (fall) season occurs between summer and winter.

BALLING
When flower buds fail to open, usually because the petals become wet and stick together. A wet-weather problem.

BUD UNION
This is the point where the bud and rootstock are joined.

BUDDING
The grafting of a bud into the neck of a rootstock. A propagation method used in commercial production.

BUTTON EYE
This is where petals are folded inwards to form a button in the centre of the bloom. It is a characteristic of some old-fashioned varieties.

DIE-BACK
A progressive dying back of the stems from the tips.

GARDEN/YARD
A plot of land available for personal use.

GRAFTING
The joining of a stem or bud of one plant onto the stem of another.

GREEN FINGERS/GREEN THUMB
A natural ability at gardening.

HOSEPIPE/(GARDEN) HOSE
Used to distribute water, either from a reserve or tap.

LADYBIRD/LADYBUG
A small beetle, often red with black spots. The purpose of their colouring is to ward off predators.

MULCH
A layer of organic matter placed around bushes to conserve moisture in the soil, prevent the germination of weed seed and to contribute nutrients to the plant.

PANICLE
A branched cluster of flowers.

PATIO/COURTYARD
A paved area of land which can often be made of bricks, tiles, cobble or gravel.

QUARTERED
This is a term often used to describe the unfolding shape of certain flowers, which appear to have four segments or quarters to the unfolding bloom.

ROOTSTOCK
This is the host root system of the plant onto which the selected cultivated variety will be budded.

SCION
A bud used for grafting onto the rootstock.

SPORT
A plant that shows mutation from its original parent.

SUCKER
A shoot that appears from below ground, which grows directly from the rootstock.

TRUSS
A number of flowers on one stem.

Garden owner and designer credits

10: t: Sissinghurst Castle Garden, The National Trust. 15: Great Dixter, Christopher Lloyd. 27: br: Glebe Cottage, Carol Klein. 31: t: Perch Hill, Sarah Raven. 36: Great Dixter, Christopher Lloyd. 37: Ashwood Nurseries, John Massey. 42: Lower Hopton Farm, Veronica Cross. 46: r: Glebe Cottage, Carol Klein. 49: Great Dixter, Christopher Lloyd. 84: t: Hidcote Manor Garden, The National Trust. 89: Great Dixter, Christopher Lloyd. 91: t: Cotswold Garden Flowers, Bob Brown. 106: l: Private Garden, Alan Titchmarsh. 119: tr: Perch Hill, Sarah Raven; 2nd from tr: Sissinghurst Castle Garden, The National Trust. 125: Great Dixter, Christopher Lloyd. 135: The Old Rectory, Mary Keen. 150/151: Glebe Cottage, Carol Klein. 158: Perch Hill, Sarah Raven. 160: Well Cottage, Joe Swift & Sam Joyce. 188: r: Sissinghurst Castle Garden, The National Trust. 190: t: Cotswold Garden Flowers, Bob Brown. 208: Old Barn, Bob Brown. 213: r: Great Dixter, Christopher Lloyd.

PICTURE CREDITS

Photographs by Jonathan Buckley other than those stated below.

b = bottom   t = top   l = left   r = right   f = far   m = middle

All images preceded with an asterix have been supplied by GAP Photos - www.gapphotos.com.

2/3: *Christa Brand
8: t: *Howard Rice
9: b: *John Glover;
   t: *Jonathan Need
10: b: *Jerry Harpur
11: t: Travel Ink/Getty
images;
   b: Danita Delimont/
Getty Images
12/13: *Elke Borkowski
16: *Nicola Stocken
17: bl: *Amy Vonheim;
   tl: *Matteo
Carassale
19: bl: *Christa Brand
21: b: Clive Nichols
23: b: *Richard Bloom
27: bl: *Nicola Stocken;
   tl: *Christa Brand
29: *Carole Drake
32: b: *Dave Zubraski;
   t: *Ron Evans
33: b: Nick Bailey;
   t: Clive Nichols
35: *Nicola Stocken
38: bl: *Paul Debois
40/41: *Elke Borkowski
44: l: *Tommy Tonsberg
45: *J S Sira

50: r: *Victoria Firmston
51: *Richard Loader
52: r: *Nicola Stocken;
   l: *Richard Bloom
53: l: *Howard Rice
57: l: *John Glover
58: m: *Richard Bloom;
   l: *Visions;
   r: *Jan Smith
59: *Neil Holmes
60/61: *Christa Brand
62: *Heather Edwards
72: m: *Thomas Alamy;
   l: *Charles Hawes
73: m: *Victoria
Firmston
75: *Clive Nichols
80: *Heather Edwards
81: b: *Howard Rice;
   t: *Nicola Stocken
82/83: *Oliver Mathews
85: br: *Richard Bloom
86: b: *Carole Drake;
   t: *Matt Anker
87: l: *Jo Whitworth
88: br: *Howard Rice;
   tl: *Visions;
   bl: *Visions
90: b: *Nicola Stocken

93: tl: *Martin Staffler;
   tr: *Maxine Adcock
94: b: *Mark Bolton;
   t: *Richard Bloom
96/97: *Christa Brand
99: l: *Howard Rice
100: l: *Visions
102: l: *Howard Rice
105: r: *Lynn Keddie
109: l: Thompson &
Morgan;
   r: *Friedrich
Strauss;
   m: *Matt Anker
110: *Carole Drake
113: *Christa Brand
114: r: Clive Nichols;
   fl: *Gerald
Majumdar;
   mr: *Dianna
Jazwinski
115: *Matt Anker
116/117: *Nicola
Stocken
118: *Nicola Stocken
119: r 2nd from b:
*Geoff Kidd;
   rb: *Thomas Alamy
120: Thompson &

Morgan;
   rt: *Richard Loader
123: bl: *Neil Overy
124: t: Crocus;
   lm: *Joanna Kossak
126/127: *Elke
Borkowski
128: *Manuela Goehner
129: t: *Dianna Jazwinski
130: b: *J S Sira
133: t: *Visions
136: *Howard Rice
137: b: *Tommy
Tonsberg;
   t: *Rob Whitworth
141: Nick Bailey;
   tl: *Jason Ingram;
   tr: *Annette
Lepple
142: bl: *Julie
Dansereau;
   br: *Fiona Mcleod
143: r: *Pernilla
Bergdahl
144: t: *Maayke de
Ridder;
   t: *Joanna Kossak;
   br: *Howard Rice;
   bl: *Joanna Kossak

148: Nick Bailey;
   tl: *Howard Rice
153: l: *John Glover;
   r: *Fiona Lea
157: l: *Howard Rice
161: m: *Howard Rice
163: *Elke Borkowski
164: *Christina Bollen
165: l: *Neil Holmes
166: r: *Matteo
Carassale;
   l: *Howard Rice
167: Nick Bailey
169: l: John Hiorns
170/171: *Pernilla
Bergdahl
173: *Elke Borkowski
174: bl: *Thomas
Alamy;
   bm: *GAP Photos;
   tr: *Tim Gainey;
   tm: *Gap Photos;
   br: *Heather
Edwards
179: br: *Graham
Strong;
   t: *Richard Bloom
180/181: *Nicola
Stocken

182: *Geoff Kidd
183: tr: *Richard
Loader;
   m: *Friedrich
Strauss
186: tl: *Tim Gainey
187: r: *Richard Bloom
188: rt: *Gerald
Majumdar;
   rb: *Dave Zubraski
194/195: *Richard
Bloom
196: *Lee Avison
197: r: *Lee Avison;
   l: *GAP Photos
198: *Carole Drake
200: r: *Sabina Ruber
201: r: John Hiorns;
   l: *Richard Loader
204: l: Rex May/Alamy;
   m: *Howard Rice
206: l: *Maxine Adcock
209: r: *Clive Nichols
210: l: Crocus;
   r: *Carole Drake
211: *Rob Whitworth
213: l: *Joanna Kossak

DEDICATION

For the Believers: Kemal Mehdi, Orcillia Oppenheimer, Sarah Plumbly, Dick Scott, Ivan Tatum, Rosie Atkins and Chris Brickell.

ACKNOWLEDGEMENTS

Huge thanks to:

Alan Gray and Graham Robeson of East Ruston Old Vicarage in Norfolk for allowing us to photograph their extraordinary gardens and clever colour combinations in pots, beds and borders.

The Garden House in Devon, Great Dixter in Sussex, Narborough Hall in Norfolk and Sissinghurst Castle in Sussex for photography of their beautiful borders and plantings.

The Honourable Alistair Keith and Wing Keith for allowing us to photograph the numerous plantings I created in the gardens of their Norfolk estate.

John and Eileen at Dunbheagan for access to and photography of their richly planted garden.

Jonathan Buckley for consistently beautiful pictures and great company on lengthy shoots.

The amazing growers and breeders at David Howard Nurseries, West Acre Nurseries, David Austin Roses, Peter Beales Roses, Coblands, The Plantsmans Preference, Blooms of Bressingham, Crocus and Beth Chatto Gardens for advice and plant material.

Simon Lockyer (Lockyer Nurseries) for providing exquisite plant material.

My supportive editor Judith Hannam and the rest of the editorial team at Kyle Books.

David and Claudia Harding for allowing me to consistently evolve and develop their London garden.

Chelsea Physic Garden for support in this venture and photography on site along with Nell Jones and Kate Wilkinson for consistently holding the fort.

Christopher Bailes (former Curator, CPG) for his support in me writing the book and Rosemary Alexander (Principle EGS) for ongoing counsel.

Simon Pyle, former Vice Principle of The English Garden School, an extraordinary and truly supportive friend who is missed by all who loved him.

Lloyd Bailey and Rose Lowe for support and use of the 'writing room' at Walnut Cottage.

Valanna Qualie for fruit cakes, counsel and diligent proof reading.

Katy Willimer and Veronika Rasickaite for unswerving support and keeping me on track.

An Hachette UK Company
www.hachette.co.uk

First published in Great Britain in 2015. This edition published in 2022 by Kyle Books, an imprint of Octopus Publishing Group Limited
Carmelite House, 50 Victoria Embankment
London EC4Y 0DZ

10 9 8 7 6 5 4 3 2 1

ISBN 978 1 91423 966 3

Text © 2015 and 2022 Nick Bailey
Design and layout © 2022 Octopus Publishing Group Limited
Photographs © 2015 Jonathan Buckley (except for photographs listed on page 223)

Publishing Director: Judith Hannam
Copy Editor: Helena Caldon
Editorial Assistant: Hannah Coughlin
Designer: Jenny Semple
Photographer: Jonathan Buckley
Production: Lisa Pinnell

A Cataloguing in Publication record for this title is available from the British Library.

Colour reproduction by F1, London.